D1721172

# LIVING
## ON THIRD STREET

### PLAYS OF THE LIVING THEATRE
### 1989-1992

# LIVING
## ON THIRD STREET

**PLAYS OF THE LIVING THEATRE**
**1989–1992**

HANON REZNIKOV

EDITED BY CINDY ROSENTHAL

AUTONOMEDIA

This publication is made possible in part with public funds
from the New York State Council on the Arts, a state agency.

Thanks to Erika Biddle and James Trimarco
for design and production assistance.

Autonomedia
POB 568 Williamsburgh Station
Brooklyn, New York 11211-0568 USA

info@autonomedia.org
www.autonomedia.org

Printed in the United States

# TABLE OF CONTENTS

     Essay by Hanon Reznikov / Performance text adapted
     for the theatre by Hanon Reznikov, from poems
     by Armand Schwerner / Excerpt from Judith Malina's diary /
     Excerpt from a dialogue between Schwerner and Reznikov

     Essay by Hanon Reznikov / Performance text
     a collective creation of The Living Theatre

     Essay by Hanon Reznikov / Excerpts from
     Judith Malina's diary / Essay by Beate Bennett

     Essay by Hanon Reznikov / Performance text a collective
     creation of The Living Theatre

     Essay by Hanon Reznikov

# LIST OF FIGURES

# DEDICATION

*To the company of incandescent souls
whose art, commitment and hard work
brought The Living Theatre on Third Street
to life…*

HANON REZNIKOV, 1950—2008
With Judith Malina, Living Theatre co-director and his wife.
*[Photo: The Living Theatre Archive]*

# FOREWORD
## JAMES REZNICK

When I was asked if I would like to contribute a forward to my brother Hanon's book, I never imagined that the request would come on the day of his funeral. Despite still reeling from the blow of his untimely death and the surreality of it, I instinctively, almost enthusiastically agreed to do it, perhaps as a way to express thoughts that heretofore had been silent, or dormant.

Our history, of course, goes back to the days growing up in the East New York section of Brooklyn in the late 50's. It was a happy time, with strong memories of family gatherings, Prospect Park, stoop ball, The Brooklyn Museum, Brighton Beach, and P.S 273. Mostly, though, was the constancy of mom and dad. They were there for us through it all, always so very proud of my precocious brother and his intellectual gifts, and me for my good nature and easy smile. Moving to Long Beach (Long Island) in 1962, I vividly recall my brother and me dancing together in our new bedroom upon arriving, finally having reached suburban paradise. I remember the long summer nights, backyard barbecues, swimming in the bay, picnics on the beach, playing in the big snowdrifts around the house, and all those school memories, both his and mine. You see, being younger by four and a half years, I lived vicariously through Hanon's experiences, to the extent I shared in them. But the reality was that he wanted me to share in his experiences! He loved motivating me to learn. Not just teaching me this or that about science or history or whatever, but impressing upon me how wonderful the learning process really was. Hanon had an uncanny ability for succinct thought and expression. He could reduce a discussion or argument on a complex subject to its bare essence, the result of which might be a keen insight, or perhaps it would leave him frustrated that one could not follow his line of reasoning. Even during those early years, one could see how he began to hone his creative talent for writing and artistic expression, even his politics. I didn't realize it until much later, but those long bedtime discussions we had about family, life and the universe were clearly a prelude.

Over the years, as Hanon and I became increasingly separated by both distance and ideology, there remained a strong force pulling us together. He, probably more than I, always tried to maintain a sense of family identity for which I admired and respected him. He enjoyed sharing details of our ancestry, for which he had both a passion and reverence. Exactly how he discovered some of those details still puzzles me to this day! Of course, as with most families, there were the inevitable tensions. But despite arguments that at times reached titanic proportions with our parents, my brother was steadfast in his gratitude, love and admiration for them. After their passing, we spoke often of them, and I always felt that he harbored a deeper pain than he wanted to show. Hanon had a special affection for my Argentine wife Ti, and loved speaking with her in Italian, always calling her his "angelo." She had an ability, unlike anyone else, to bring out his softer side, for which I will forever be grateful. He was certainly very proud of his brother the doctor, but was almost equally proud that I had mastered Spanish, and therefore could welcome me into the multilingual club!

When Hanon told me recently that he was working on a book about The Living Theater's experience on Third Street, I remembered thinking 'how typical of my brother!' That as much as he was focused on the future, working on projects aimed at changing the world through theater and art, he was inevitably drawn to the past, to understanding where he came from and where he had been. Hanon had long recognized how critical an understanding and a sense of history were in developing his world view and approach to it. I cannot help but think that our own father, having been both a student and teacher of history, was highly significant in developing that strong sense in my brother.

But Judith, Hanon's wife, was clearly the most powerful and influential force in my brother's life. She combined all of the elements of wife, lover, companion, teacher, student, colleague and icon in one. Their relationship was as complex as it was real, and was a source of admiration and inspiration for all that knew them. They were an example of love's possibilities.

In the years to come, I will think of Hanon in many ways: his enthusiasm and incredible energy, at times despite medical adversity; his quick wit and humor with which he could instantly lighten a heavy situation; his infatuation with Europe but his eternal love for New York; his brilliant writings; his pride in sharing with me The Living Theater's accolades; and others way too numerous to recount here. His influence on my own life was enormous. He has left a huge void that I will never be able to fill. We shared with each other all the high moments of our lives and he was always there for me as a strong voice of calm and reassurance during the difficult times. He has left us much, much too soon. I loved him deeply and will miss him. I pray that the "angelos" are watching over him.

James Reznick
June 21, 2008
Newport Beach, CA

# PREFACE
## CINDY ROSENTHAL

Body.

❀ ❀ ❀ ❀ ❀

Physical. The lost body rediscovered. The body numbed by the industrial society. The body clamped shut by capitalistic morality, the body screwed by poverty. The body liberated by the food and poetry of revolutions. The body alive in action.

As if in the course of this play we confront the social problem which is haunting the community in the post revolutionary world: How to get out of this envelope that is encasing us and into the next.

— Julian Beck, *the life of the theatre* (1972) #32, 59-60. From a xeroxed hand-out created by company member Ilion Troya for LT actors and homeless people on the first day of rehearsal for *The Body of God* (February 14, 1990).

*The Body of God*, produced in 1990, is one of eight unique, collaborative performances featured in this book, which documents the efforts of The Living Theatre to forge bonds and open the doors of understanding between the company and its neighboring community during its four years on Third Street in New York City. LT co-director Hanon Reznikov expressed special pride in the company's community-based performance work; we both eagerly anticipated the publication of this volume, which brings the oeuvre of this lesser-known period in the history of The Living Theatre to light. On May 3, 2008, at age 57, Hanon Reznikov died of pneumonia following a stroke, a sudden and terrible loss. It is in his honor and memory that I now bring forth this important collection of essays and plays of the Third Street Theater. These works stand as a testament to Reznikov's crucial legacy in the long life of The Living Theatre, but in fact, only cover a small portion of his significant contributions as company member under Julian Beck's and Judith Malina's leadership and as co-director with Malina, since Beck's death in 1985. Over the past several years as I worked on this volume with Reznikov, I witnessed his generosity, his deep and wide-ranging knowledge, intelligence, and attention to detail, his dedication to the Living's long-sought-after goals of pacifism and anarchism, and his imagination, creativity, and strength in the face of financial and political crises as the company traveled and performed in theatres and on the street throughout the US, in Europe, and in the Middle East. *Living on Third Street: Plays of The Living Theatre 1989–1992* was very dear to Hanon's heart. It is extremely sad not to be celebrating its publication with him.

The Living Theatre was founded in 1947 in New York City by Julian Beck and Judith Malina, and from that time forward, the company has struggled (often with seemingly insurmountable financial difficulties) to maintain an ongoing presence and a home in New York. After closing the Third Street Theatre in 1992, it wasn't until 2007 that co-directors Malina and Reznikov were once again able to re-establish a new home at 19–21 Clinton Street, on New York's Lower East Side. It is therefore of great importance that documents of the Third Street Theatre — a highly productive, albeit brief period in The Living Theatre's history — become available to students, researchers, and practitioners of contemporary avant-garde performance. These texts cast new light on recurrent themes and concerns of the pacifist/anarchist theatre collective in its continuing efforts to cultivate an ensemble and a body of work that speak to pressing issues of today.

Reznikov became co-director of The Living Theatre with Malina after Beck's death from cancer in 1985. *Living on Third Street* affords the reader an opportunity to analyze the impact of this shift at the center of The Living Theatre's collectivity, as it chronicles Reznikov's work as playwright, performer, and co-director/inspirator with Judith Malina. In addition to the five performance texts in this volume, all written or co-created by Reznikov (available to scholars and practitioners for the first time), the photographs, song sheets, design sketches, interviews, essays, and diary excerpts from associate artists and company members, as well as the book's appendix, with a chronological list of the performance events at the theatre, provide a detailed, multi-faceted record of the creative vitality and the diversity of forms, styles, and artists inside the Third Street Theatre. The interconnections between this work and the often-tumultuous scene on the streets and in the community outside the theatre also become abundantly clear. The East Village, and specifically "alphabet city" (the Third Street Theatre was located between Avenues C and D), were at an apex of cultural and political activity in the late 1980s and early 1990s.

*Tumult, or Clearing the Streets* and *The Body of God*, two of the eight works produced during 1989–1992 (see Chapters 2 and 4), were emblematic of a current trend in Living Theatre practice: creative collaboration with a community that involves direct engagement with important issues in that community. *Tumult* (August 5, 1989–September 2, 1989) was a street theatre work presented in the East Village, in Brooklyn, and in Staten Island, which argued for the right to use public spaces. Central themes in *Tumult* were community gardeners' rights to protect and preserve community gardens, squatter's rights, and the right to assemble peacefully in streets and parks (the 1988 riots in the East Village's Tompkins Square Park were a focal point in the text). *The Body of God* concerned the problems of housing and homelessness. This play was a "collective creation" developed by homeless people, squatters, activists, and Living Theatre members.

For East Village residents in 1989 (as well as today) problems of housing, of the use of public space, and of environmental racism were/are of primary concern. The plays above, which centered on these issues, point to a significant moment in the Living's development of an identity, ideology, and aesthetic as a community-based theatre. Since The Living Theatre's first foray into street theatre and community-based work in 1970, in the shanty towns of Brazil, the group has been struggling with contradictory impulses: its need to create "a theatre of change" that will have a clear impact on its spectators because it speaks directly to, with, and for those spectators, and its desire to create a public presence that will bring in the audiences and the income the company so desperately needs. In 1989, five years after Beck's death and nearly two decades after he wrote the Marxist-influenced manifesto in the life of the theatre excerpted above, The Living Theatre, under Malina's and Reznikov's direction, took up the challenge "to confront the social problem" locally and directly on Third Street. Thirteen years later, on August 19, 2002, after nearly two decades of struggle, including fiery, sometimes violent confrontations between squatters and police, NYC (under Mayor Michael R. Bloomberg's administration) began the historic process of transferring eleven buildings on the Lower East Side to their squatters as low-cost co-ops. Squatters' rights were a focus of both *Tumult* and *The Body of God*.

Another key issue affecting the East Village in 1989–92 was the fate of community gardens, which was also a central theme in *Tumult*. The Living Theatre's interest in establishing and preserving community gardens grew out of a project entitled *Turning the Earth*, which The Living Theatre produced the summer before (1988) in vacant lots throughout the city — in the East Village, Staten Island, Brooklyn, and Harlem. This performance work, which was based on Native American planting rituals, grew out of *The Legacy of Cain* cycle of street plays, which were first produced in the US in Pittsburgh, PA in 1975.

NYC community gardens, located in all five boroughs, many in neighborhoods of color with little access to other green, open space, were on the city's books as vacant lots. As locals began to homestead in abandoned buildings on the Lower East Side, NYC gardeners began to "squat" in empty lots — cleaning them up and planting trees, vegetables, and flowers — and transforming these spaces into community gathering places that helped revitalize the neighborhoods. Since the mid 1980s the city had tried to reclaim the lots for housing development and gardeners fought back to preserve these few green spaces. On September 18, 2002, Bloomberg and New York State Attorney General Eliot Spitzer signed a landmark agreement guaranteeing the preservation of 198 gardens that had been marked as potential sites for development and established a "garden review process" that laid out an equitable time frame and procedure for making a case for a garden's preservation.

Working with local artists, activists, and residents, the Living created *Tumult* in its first summer on Third Street. Company member Joanie Fritz Zosike, who did not perform in *Tumult* but saw the piece several times, described it as particularly striking because of its fast-moving processions, its ornate, sculptural body formations, and its pageantry. (See the *Tumult* photos in this volume.) *Tumult* fits Jan Cohen-Cruz's description of agit-prop street theatre (1998, 5, 13) which includes "emblematic costumes and props [and] choral speaking" designed to simplify and theatricalize its "partisan points of view" in order "to capture by-passers' attention." Co-director Malina told me that a goal of the Living's street theatre is to "create plays that can speak on many levels to many people" (1998).

How (clearly) a performance speaks to a group or groups of people, and how the efficacy of a performance is measured and assessed continues to be of seminal interest and concern to scholars and practitioners of radical theatre. Baz Kershaw re-frames the efficacy question in his *Politics of Performance* (1992, 3), suggesting that paying "more attention to the conditions of performance that are most likely to produce an efficacious result" is a viable alternative to the empirical research approach some scholars have attempted. Kershaw's idea of focusing on "the potential of performance to achieve efficacy in a particular historical context," is useful in analyzing The Living Theatre's Third Street work.

Describing the Living's role in the anarchist movements in the East Village, Malina emphasized that "the most important thing is that The Living Theatre was there, was open, during and after the struggle for Tompkins Square Park" (located between Avenues A and B, and between East 7th Street and East 10th Street). Demonstrators supporting the tent-dwellers in Tompkins Square Park and the homesteaders in the nearby squats clashed violently with the police in and around Tompkins Square Park on August 6 and 7, 1988. Arguably it was this clash that motivated the company's intense interest in the storefront space on Third Street. The Living chose to make the East Village its home, realizing that this was a neighborhood where direct action theatre was most needed. *Tu-*

*mult* opened a day before the one-year anniversary of the riots, in Prospect Park, Brooklyn, on August 5, 1989. Clayton Patterson, a videographer who had documented the riots, told me:

> The Living Theatre came in as an outside entity, but almost like a mussel under a ship, it attached itself to the movement. The Living Theatre worked itself into the community; it became a force, a meeting place. There were only a few meeting places like that, and no other theatres. La Mama was totally out of it; Theatre for the New City was not consistently involved. Certainly not PS 122. But the Living got involved. The Living Theatre showed up.

Reznikov's adaptation of Armand Schwerner's *The Tablets* (see Chapter 1) was the first LT play produced at Third Street (opened May 26, 1989). Spectators were meant to identify with and examine the central Scholar/Translator role in the piece, a figure who confronts the challenge of understanding the roots of our human condition. Reznikov contends that here "this mystery can best be explored through the dimension of poetry." *The Tablets* takes the form of an "inward-looking research project" Reznikov explains (2004).

*The Body of God*, on the other hand, can be seen as the play that figuratively opened the doors of the theatre (first performance March 28, 1990) to the most marginalized among us, the homeless. "You couldn't be in that neighborhood and not get involved with the homeless cause," Fritz Zosike told me (2002). Homeless people slept at the front door of the storefront theatre space each night. According to another company member, Lois Kagan Mingus, "We talked, as a company, of what we wanted to do in that space and it was so obvious to all of us. We knew we didn't want to point a finger at it — yes, that's homelessness — or talk about it, and as a bunch of actors portray it. Let's let the people who are experiencing it now *be* it. That's the way we'll tell the story" (2002). The Living Theatre's production of *The Body of God* contains a central, ten-minute section devoted to small group discussions among audience members and performers on the subjects of money, homelessness, and squatters' rights. Other sections consist of movement, music, poetry, dramatic monologues, and sermon-like renditions of the stories of homeless people, who, with an equal number of Living Theatre actors, squatters, and activists, performed these pieces. For the Living, the goals were clear: to change the thinking about, behaviors towards, and ultimately, the material conditions affecting homeless people in NYC. And although the play was staged inside the theatre, the material conditions of the theatre experience were radically changed too (see Chapter 4).

*Village Voice* critic Roderick Mason Faber described *The Body of God* as "a moving audience-participatory work, which focuses not only on the sensuous immediacy of the theatrical event at hand, but also on the harrowing plight of the people who live on the streets outside.... It is above all a call to action." In her review, *Villager* critic Sarah Tittle described her participation in "The Chord" (a Living Theatre audience participation technique first used in *Mysteries and Smaller Pieces*, 1964) at the end of *The Body of God* as "unorchestrated and exciting. It's what happens when people work at something together." Tittle's and Faber's spectator accounts reflect Fritz Zosike's, and Kagen-Mingus's views of *The Body of God*, bringing to mind Victor Turner's concept of *communitas*, and a community cohesiveness along ideological lines that Kershaw suggests may be potentially powerful, even if the political efficacy is "slow-burning" (1992, 28). The success of the production led to its re-creation a year later with many of the same homeless participants, as well as some new to the project.

Patterson and The Living Theatre members I've talked with over the past few years look back with wistfulness and pride on the 1989–92 period. Fritz Zosike pointed out local activist/artists, like Michael Shenker, a musician, performer, and the composer of *Waste* (a Living Theatre street performance produced 1991–92, see Chapter 7), who was featured in several media accounts (the *Village Voice*, the *New York Times*) addressing the city's "new deal" for squatters. Ultimately, we don't know whether legislative aides or politicians picked up reviews or were in the audience of *The Body of God*; we cannot know who was on the street when *Tumult* catapulted by. Some homeless people and squatters' lives were changed, however, and Third Street activists and artists were foregrounded by the media. Although "the slow burning fuse of efficacy may be invisible," as Kershaw put it, the heat produced over time can have a perceptible and even a significant impact on the ideologies of a community. *Living on Third Street* documents what may be regarded as a "hot" and until now, unexamined period in radical theatre and performance history.

WORKS CITED

Cohen-Cruz, Jan. *Radical Street Performance*. London and New York: Routledge, 1998.
Faber, Roderick Mason. "The Body of God." *The Village Voice*. November 20, 1990, p. 114.
Fritz Zosike, Joanie. Phone interview with the author, September 26, 2002.
Kagan Mingus, Lois. Interview with the author, September 18, 2002.
Kershaw, Baz. *The Politics of Performance: Radical Theatre as Cultural Intervention*. London and New York: Routledge, 1992.
Malina, Judith. From an interview with the author published in "Living on the Street" in *Radical Street Performance*, pp. 151, 159.
Patterson, Clayton. Interview with the author, September 24, 2002.
Reznikov, Hanon. Conversation with the author, April 16, 2004.
Tittle, Sarah. "*Body of God* Brings the Audience Closer to Homelessness." *The Villager*. April 19, 1990, p. 8.

# INTRODUCTION

Setting down the chronicle of what went on at Third Street is a bittersweet pleasure for me — sweet to consider how much we accomplished and bitter to recount the nasty realities that have prevented us from holding onto a space. But my real purpose in these pages is to present an accounting of a remarkably fertile period in the half-century-long life of The Living Theatre. It can hardly be an objective evaluation, since I was personally responsible as producer, director and/or author of all the productions under consideration, but then, pretensions of objectivity by even the most distanced of observers are nowadays understood to be suspect. My history with the company dates from our first encounter in 1968 at Yale, the scene of The Living Theatre's first U.S. performances since their exile began five years earlier. Soon after, I changed my major from Molecular Biophysics to Drama, got some experience at acting and directing, and then arrived at their doorstep in 1973.

What I will try to do in these pages is to share with the reader the particularizing details of the creation and presentation of The Living Theatre's work from 1989 to 1992. Rather than restrict the book to narrative, description and commentary, co-editor Cindy Rosenthal has helped to collect a broad range of original materials — fertile period and so on — intended to give the reader a chance to examine the work first-hand, or as close to that as is possible in a book.

The format here is chronological, beginning with a resumé of the four decades of Living Theatre history leading up to Third Street, and then examining each of nine of the company's principal productions during the period in question: *The Tablets, Tumult — or Clearing the Streets, I and I, The Body of God, German Requiem, Rules of Civility, Waste, The Zero Method* and *Echoes of Justice.* We will make all-too-brief mention of the many other plays and events of all kinds — poetry and play readings, dance and music concerts, community and political meetings, exhibitions and more — that made The Living Theatre on Third Street the "total theater" it was.

In 1943 Judith Malina and Julian Beck were introduced in New York, fell in love with each other and with the idea of a theatre dedicated to high art of the modernist kind. Malina enrolled in Erwin Piscator's newly founded Dramatic Workshop at the New School.

The place was a creative hotspot. Malina's fellow students included Beatrice Arthur, Harry Belafonte, Marlon Brando, Walter Matthau, Gene Saks, Bernard Schwartz (Tony Curtis), Jerry Stiller, Elaine Strich and Tennessee Williams. Piscator himself, John Gassner, Paolo Milano and Paul Zucker taught theory; the acting department was led by Lee Strasberg and Stella Adler. At the same time, Julian was a promising young painter of the abstract expressionist persuasion, exhibiting at Peggy Guggenheim's seminal 57th Street gallery, *Art of this Century*. Their circle included John Cage and Merce Cunningham, Jack Kerouac and Allen Ginsberg, Frank O'Hara and John Ashbery, Willem De Kooning and Robert Motherwell, Helen Frankenthaler and Clement Greenberg, Jack Smith and Ray Johnson, Joseph Campbell and Jean Erdman, Erick Hawkins and Lucia Dlugoszewski, William Carlos Williams and W.H. Auden, Robert Edmond Jones and e.e. cummings, Anaïs Nin and James Agee, Fritz Perls and Paul Goodman, and scores of the other creative minds busily renovating Western culture. The Living Theatre was born in the bosom of this postwar New York modernist movement and was understood by artists of all kinds to be their theater.

Falling afoul of the authorities from the very beginning — their first attempt in the late forties to open a performing space in a basement in pre-SoHo Wooster Street was blocked by the local precinct, which called the enterprise a front for prostitution because, the police said, a newspaper advertisement for "actors and actresses" such as Julian and Judith had placed could refer only to an illicit enterprise, since artists were unknown on Wooster Street. Frustrated by the fruitless search for a space, Julian and Judith decided in 1951 to make their West End Aveunue living room the arena for the first Living Theatre program, a compendium of short plays including Bertolt Brecht's *He Who Says Yes and He Who Says No*, Garcia Lorca's *The Dialogue of the Young Man and the Mannekin*, Paul Goodman's *Childish Jokes* and Gertrude Stein's *Ladies' Voices*. Later that same year they signed a lease on the Cherry Lane Theater in Greenwich Village, where they presented Stein (*Doctor Faustus Lights the Lights*), Rexroth (*Beyond the Mountains*), Goodman (*Faustina*), Ashbery (*The Heroes*), Eliot (*Sweeney Agonistes*), Picasso (*Desire Trapped by the Tail*), Jarry (*Ubu Roi*) among others. And it was there at the Cherry Lane that The Living Theatre also began to sponsor events by other artists — poetry readings, for instance (Dylan Thomas was one) and concerts (John Cage was another) which did much to reinforce the artists' sense of themselves as a community with The Living Theatre at its center. In 1953 The Living Theatre at the Cherry Lane Theater was closed by the Fire Department. The next year, Julian and Judith rented a loft on Broadway at 100th Street where for two years they presented a new series of experiments, including plays by Strindberg (*The Spook Sonata*), Racine (*Phèdre*), Auden (*The Age of Anxiety*), Cocteau (*Orpheus*), Pirandello (*Tonight We Improvise*), and Goodman (*The Young Disciple*). In 1956, the Buildings Department ruled that the loft space could not legally hold more than 18 people and so on they searched until in 1958 they found an abandoned department store on the corner of 14th Street and Sixth Avenue, and reopened it as The Living Theatre with a staging of William Carlos Williams' *Many Loves*. It was an auspicious beginning, but it was their later productions of Jack Gelber's *The Connection* and Ken Brown's *The Brig* that first brought them international attention. In 1963, The Living Theatre on 14th Street was closed by the I.R.S. While the trial verdict was that the theater owed no taxes, the closing catalyzed the company's transformation into a nomadic, tribal group, and earned Julian and Judith 60-day and 30-day prison sentences, respectively, for contempt of court, that is, for conducting themselves at the trial as the directors of the theatrical proceedings.

Moving about through Europe the company — which during its first two European tours in the early sixties had already excited the intelligentsia in London, Paris, Rome and Berlin as the most cutting edge of avant-garde theaters — began to create a new repertory, living and working collectively and discovering entirely novel forms of theatrical expression in such works as *Mysteries and smaller pieces, Frankenstein* and *Paradise Now*. These productions were so radically different in form and intention from other contemporary theater works that they spawned a whole new generation of theatre ensembles experimenting in similar directions. The company returned to America for a coast-to-coast tour of these epoch-making works in 1968–69, radicalizing the lives of many among the audiences they encountered along the way. Mine was one of them.

For most of the 1970's the group concentrated on plays performed outside traditional venues, creating a cycle of dozens of plays collectively called *The Legacy of Cain*. These productions, which included *Seven Meditations on Political Sado-Masochism, The Money Tower, Six Public Acts, Turning the Earth* and the *Strike Support Oratorium*, were designed for streets, factory gates and lunchrooms, schools, hospitals and other non-theatrical venues. The project began in earnest in 1970 in Brazil, where after a year of interaction with the *favelados*, or shantytown dwellers, the company was imprisoned for two and a half months on charges of subversion until worldwide protests embarrassed the military government into deporting them back to New York. The project then continued with a year's residence in Pittsburgh, where the company targeted both industrial workers (*The Money Tower* rose at the very gates of the still-active steel mills) and the poor, mostly black population of the crumbling ghettos, where *Six Public Acts* made its processional way through the streets. There followed an even longer period of activity in Italy where The Living Theatre performed alongside striking workers occupying factories in the north as well as among the unemployed in the impoverished south.

At the close of the 1970's, the company developed a strategy to support this street theater activity by touring virtually nonstop throughout Europe, performing both in theaters and out on the street. In Italy in 1978, The Living Theatre created *Prometheus* at the Winter Palace, which marked the company's return to the stage proper. Successive stage productions included a revival of the company's 1967 staging of Bertolt Brecht's *Antigone* (Piraeus, 1979), Ernst Toller's *Masse-Mensch* (Munich, 1980), my own adaptation of the writings of Bernard Shaw and Wassily Kandinsky, called *The Yellow Methuselah* (Rome, 1982), and Julian Beck's *Archaeology of Sleep* (Nantes, 1983).

It was with this European-born repertory that The Living Theatre returned to New York in 1983 to offer a six-week run of four plays at the Joyce Theater. The Reagan-era press had nothing but contempt for these hold-overs from the sixties, defined by Frank Rich in the *New York Times* as "an undistinguished band of international riff-raff." The subsequent illness and death of Julian Beck determined a change in the company's plans. Rather than return to France and continue the group's efforts to secure a theater of its own in Paris with the support of the Ministry of Culture, Judith Malina decided to stay in New York.

European-born Malina had always had a preference for New York even as New York-born Beck preferred Europe. She believed, further, that the chemistry for political change was right in New York, that the contradictions of capitalism would reach a flashpoint here, and that here the coming crisis would be of worldwide significance.

At this point, The Living Theatre's journey became again a New York journey that would lead to Third Street. Some months after Julian's death, the remnants of the Joyce company (the Europeans had returned to Europe) and several New York-based veterans of the sixties company (Steven Ben Israel, Gianfranco Mantegna, Mary Mary, Birgit Knabe and Pamela Badyk among them) gathered in a circle with Malina at the Bleecker Street gallery where Julian's wondrous drawings from the forties and fifties were on display, floated within brightly-lit frame-boxes. There they performed a theatrical ritual animated by his dazzling, long poem, "Daily Light." Julian would have been tickled to know that Leo Castelli was in the audience. It was a kind of reconsecration of the company and a few months later, Judith began work on another transitional project, a staging of Karen Malpede's *Us*, a 2-actor/6-character study of two lovers and their abusive parents, at the new home of Theater for the New City on First Avenue at 10th Street. George Bartenieff and Crystal Field, directors of TNC, co-produced the show and turned in phenomenal performances as the sextet of characters (Bartenieff had been in *The Brig* on 14th Street and as a teenager, he had also played Pinocchio to Malina's Cat at Piscator's Dramatic Workshop). Ilion Troya, a Brazilian member of the company since their sojourn there in 1970–71, designed a constructivist set that fulfilled Malina's Meyerholdian stage-plan superbly. The following March, the company rented space at Charas, an ex-school turned community cultural center just east of Tompkins Square Park, where we created *Poland/1931*, a seven-actor staging of Jerome Rothenberg's epic cycle of poems about the lives of Esther K. (Malina) and Leo Levy (WBAI radio personality Bob Fass) which I adapted and directed.

Later that year (1988), Malina directed Michael McClure's *VKTMS: Orestes in Scenes* at Theater for the New City. I played Orestes; Tom Walker (who, like me, had met The Living Theatre at Yale in 1968) was Pylades; Julie Sukman, a promising neophyte, was Elektra; and Sheila Dabney, a dazzlingly accomplished actor, was Helen.

During these years following the death of Julian, Judith and I cemented our many years of loving partnership into a marriage and co-directorship of the theater. Together we led a search for an East Village space that would constitute a real home for The Living Theatre. For a long time we looked at city-owned properties that we hoped to be able to raise enough money to buy. During this period, we obtained small grants from the city's Department of Cultural Affairs, the New York State Council on the Arts, and the National Endowment for the Arts. Year by year, these grants slowly grew and encouraged us to think that if we were to find our own space, we could increase our artistic output and obtain more funding, both from the government and from private foundations. One of our leading actors, Joanie Fritz Zosike, began working on funding possibilities and before long, Judith's daughter, Isha, would also be keeping the office humming.

The quest for space went on for quite some time. Among the buildings we considered, we had a particular interest in an abandoned synagogue on East 7th Street between Avenues B and C. Standing alone in the midst of a vacant lot, the temple was elegantly proportioned but terribly narrow for theatrical purposes (17 feet in interior width); board member and architect Percival Goodman advised against it. But there were biblical mosaics in the entryway and a tall, uplifting ceiling.... Plans of the building were obtained from the city archives, drawings of the projected renovation were drafted, a first appeal to the theater's mailing list was sent out, and a rabbi, Shlomo Carlebach, was added to the board. Shlomo's father, Naphtali, had been Judith's father's teacher in Berlin in the 20's and had visited Malina in jail in the 50's, as a chaplain, when she was doing time for a peace protest. Harvey Seifter, who had engineered Theater for the New City's acquisition of its vast new quarters from the city, was hired to do the same for us. Proposals were presented to the city's Department of Cultural Affairs, to the Department of Real Property, to the Department of Housing and Urban Development, to the community board, to the neighborhood council, to the block association. Judith and I passed long hours as supplicants in attendance at the meetings of these organizations. Finally, we learned that an evangelical church just down the street had plans of its own for that synagogue. They had been doing important and caring work in the community, sponsoring food and housing programs, which they hoped to expand into the empty temple across the street. The block association was behind them. As relative outsiders, we found ourselves in an untenable position. Even if we could, we were not willing to begin our work in this community by elbowing out a grassroots facility. Just as the synagogue fell through, Harvey Seifter left for San Francisco to become managing director of the Magic Theater.

Disappointed but not discouraged, we walked the neighborhood streets, drove around every block, looking at likely and unlikely haunts. After a time we identified a site on Allen Street, a grand old public bathhouse employed at the time by the city as a warehouse for confiscated gambling machines. It had a neo-Roman facade and was filled with scores of pink marble bath and shower stalls. South of Houston Street, this location was no longer the East Village, but the even more avant-garde and politically correct Lower East Side (there are differing definitions of the boundary). We began anew the round of inquiries, proposals, applications, meetings. We found ourselves competing again for the space with another group. This time it was the Center for Artists and Architecture, whose claim was no stronger than ours. But after reviewing the costs of acquisition and renovation, and taking a hard look at the time frame involved in negotiating with the various city agencies and departments for the purchase of the Allen Street Baths, we came to realize that a Gordian knot could be swiftly undone if we could find a commercial space at a reasonably low rent. We shifted strategy from long-term permanent acquisition, with all its attendant complications, to a simple rental.

The recession had taken its toll in the East Village real estate market; almost all of the art galleries that had mushroomed about the neighborhood in the early eighties were out of business or had moved to SoHo. So after consideration of a few alternatives, including a former fish smokehouse and an upper-story loft in a ex-furniture store, Judith and I spotted the empty store at 272 East Third Street while driving up and down the streets searching out space. The gate was down, but we could make out through the glass front that the space extended significantly into the back. We called the posted realtor's number and arranged a look inside.

This was a storefront whose rear wall boasted an arch opening onto a back room of minimally satisfactory dimensions for a 74-seat theater. The laws governing spaces rated at occupancy of 75 or greater are much more stringent, requiring sprinkler systems and so on. We also discovered that according to the building code, premises on side streets are not required to have a second means of egress if they happen to be situated within 30 feet of an avenue. And 272 East Third fit the bill. Most importantly, we liked the feel of the place. The front room, which occupied the ground floor of a four-story apartment building, would make a good-sized lobby and/or office (this "and/or" would prove a nagging problem later). The rear room, a single-story extension into the backyard with a square cupola in the middle of the ceiling, promised to make a fine little black box of a theater. Further, there was a stairway in the rear leading to a large, moldy basement that would serve as dressing room, shop and storage. The real estate agent quoted us a monthly rent of $3000. We estimated that if we could negotiate that figure down to closer to $2000 we might just be able to make it work.

We called in Sari Weisman, the real estate specialist at A.R.T./NY, a service organization for resident theaters which we had joined a year or two previously. She was immensely helpful in helping us to outline the terms of the lease and even participated in the final negotiation with the landlord. We also had the assistance of Carlo Altomare, a newly-returned member of the fold who had left ten years earlier with Mary Mary to found a new ensemble (called "MoMo" at first, and later, "The Alchemical Theater") which had recently dissolved. Several of its members had already begun to work with our company, having trained in the Artaudian and Meyerholdian basics of our style with Carlo and Mary. On April 3, 1989, Judith and I met with the landlord at his Second Avenue offices, Sari and Carlo at our side.

After perhaps an hour of rather tough negotiations, we shook on the deal. The rent was to be $2000 in the first year, with a $200/month increase each year. We were to have the right to renew in 1992 and, on my insistence, the right to walk away from the situation on 90 days' notice. Four days later we met Atkins in an Amsterdam Avenue bar he held in partnership. He ordered drinks and confided that he was really an artist who had gotten into real estate out of necessity. He now owned a dozen buildings, most of them tenements in the East Village like the one containing our storefront. "I'm getting out of residential buildings. I don't like dealing with people who can't pay the rent on their home." We handed him a certified check for $6000 (two months' rent and a month's security deposit) and he handed us the keys to 272 East Third Street. It was curious about the starting sum — $6000 was the exact amount Julian had inherited in the late 1940's with which he and Judith launched The Living Theatre.

We rushed downtown immediately, our hearts pounding as we unlocked and lifted the security gate protecting the newly-installed plate-glass storefront. We moved slowly past the archway into the mysterious gloom of the soon-to-be-a-theater chamber and sat on the floor for a few quiet minutes, our arms tight around each other. Another chapter had begun.

In the weeks that followed, as we cleaned and painted, did wiring and plumbing, we began to get to know our neighbors. The starving young artists made themselves known in short order, though the most politically correct of the young locals, many of them recent graduates of expensive schools, kept a certain distance, as we represented to them another regrettable instance of gentrification. Just a few doors down there was a municipal family shelter and right across the street, a public health facility. A news stand occupying the stretch of sidewalk between our front windows and the pawn shop on the corner was rented by a local artist, Jim C (named for the Avenue) who used it for installations. The current version consisted of strobelit styrofoam wigstands whirling on turntables against a expressionistically painted backdrop. At the eastern end of the mostly Spanish-speaking block, toward the public housing project on Avenue D (very much like the one in which I grew up in East New York), there was a performance venue called the Bullet Space. On the next block in the other direction was the very hip and successful Nuyorican Poets Café. A block further west, between Avenues A and B, was a fashionable late-night spot called Delia's, after its debutante owner. The area was chock-full of beautifully maintained community gardens sprung up in vacant lots where, during the preceding summer, in 1988, we had done a number of performances of *Turning the Earth,* a street play we first created in Pittsburgh in 1975, about the nutritive potential of urban soil. And all about the neighborhood, a number of abandoned tenements had been occupied by squatters. Some of these, like the 13th Street building that had housed the Alchemical Theater, were outfitted rather inventively. Electricity could be procured by tapping into the nearest streetlight, sometimes with the illicit cooperation of disgruntled Con Ed employees. Heating was often supplied by burning scrap wood scavenged from vacant lots in oil-drum furnaces. The toilets, typically, were bucket-flushed. LaMama was one block north, four blocks west, and lightyears upscale of us. The drug dealers were everywhere, as were the rats and roaches. We tried to get along with everybody.

Even before we began preparations for our first production, we inaugurated the space as our community's new common ground with a Passover seder. This annual ceremonial dinner in celebration of the end of slavery had been a gathering point for the extended Living Theatre family for quite a few years. The walls were hung with colorful patchwork quilts and the customary giant U of a low table (doors placed atop milk crates and cinderblocks) was surrounded with cushions. And for this wandering tribe who had not considered itself to have a home since the company was ejected from its 14th Street theater some 26 years previously, the seder was truly a celebration of the end of a long wandering. Joyous were the songs that evening; inspired, the stories told and poems read. We had arrived. But where?

Neighbors filled us in. We occupied the site of the Happy Days Bar and Grill, which had been serving the neighborhood since the end of Prohibition. Sometime in the 1960's, the popular local restaurant shut its doors, after a run-in with local racketeers who had some kind of problem with the crap shoots traditionally held in the back room. One night, a customer wandered in and told us of a night more than twenty years before when a full complement of thugs with sawed-off shotguns had forced him and his companions to strip naked and lie on the basement floor while they made off with their cash and jewelry. "There I was, lying right on top of my buddy John's girlfriend, both of us butt-naked!" he laughed hoarsely. We couldn't help but hear it as a grotesque version of the *Paradise Now* body pile. The owners took fright and closed. A couple of years later, when hip-dom had bled east deep into Alphabet City, the place reopened as The Sin Club, where off-off-off "events" were spawned. This arrangement gave way to an after-hours joint known as Stupid/Fresh, where, we were told, a patrol car would stop by at least once a night to collect a share of the proceeds.

And now it was The Living Theatre on Third Street. Certain key questions loomed large in our minds. How much would we get done here? How long would it last? What were we dealing with here?

The East Village in 1989 was a place in ferment. The "gentrification" of large stretches of the neighborhood during the boom years of the eighties had come to a virtual halt after the stock market crash of 1987. Much had already been invested in renovating newly upscale buildings such as Christadora House on Tompkins Square which had attempted to sell penthouse apartments for upwards of a million dollars. Although most of the art galleries disappeared over the ensuing years, a sizeable contingent of people with disposable income remained. The East Village and the Lower East Side with which it is contiguous were unique in the city in offering a dense concentration of artists decidedly anti-establishment in their leanings, as well as certain middle-class working people (teachers, computer wonks, advertising account execs and so on) who like to live among such artists, a rich stratum of poor people, mostly Hispanics from Puerto Rico and the Dominican Republic, and a vast supply of experimental performance venues, offbeat shops, bars and restaurants, etc. halfway between midtown and the financial district.

The neighborhood is home to a particularly vocal contingent of activists of many stripes: environmentalists, feminists, squatters, housing rights advocates, public health advocates, old guard anti-imperialists and anti-authoritarians who often call themselves anarchists (especially regrettably, when they respond in kind to violent challenges by the police).

We created theatrical projects designed to reach out to all these groups. When we were performing *Tumult, or Clearing the Streets* or *The Body of God*, plays which address the problems of housing and the use of public spaces, we were able to afford to members of the squatters' movement and to those campaigning for aid to the homeless the opportunity to address audiences directly about these concerns. When we mounted our street epic, *Waste,* we were able to involve local environmental groups. During the initial run of *Rules of Civility,* which coincided with the war in the Persian Gulf, we ended the show with a vigil in the street in coordination with War Resisters League and others voicing protest.

Our sojourn on Third Street was virtually coterminous with the George H.W. Bush administration. Thus the voices that spoke up at the theater (as they did, for instance, during audience-discussion segments of plays like *The Body of God* and *The Zero Method*) were speaking to the reality of a conservative regime in Washington whose politics it was our audience's habit to blame for most of the world's problems. It was the recessionary economic cycle, however, which, in the end, brought down public funding for social programs, for the arts, and finally, brought down the Republican White House itself.

Shortly after we moved in, Ed Koch was succeeded by David Dinkins, and ten months after we moved out, Rudy Giuliani defeated Dinkins. It was instructive to our audiences to see how ineffective such well-meaning, ostensibly progressive political leaders like Dinkins were in making any dent in the city's problems, and how such lack of progress ended in abetting the conservative "revolution," as the rightwingers so distressingly call it.

In November, 1989, five months after we moved in, the Berlin Wall fell. It was in the basement dressing room at Third Street, during a performance of

*Ian∂I*, that we gathered around the little black-and-white television with the wire-hanger antenna to witness the astonishing moments when the populace of the East scaled the wall and stood victorious atop it. I remember in particular the amazement of two of our actors, Martin Reckhaus from West Germany and Elena Jandova from Bulgaria, as we watched the ecstatic crowds surging over the Wall, in disbelief of their own situation.

How did we make a go of it economically on Third Street? Remarkably, we never did get into serious debt, despite our turning out play after play without major funding or substantial box office income. We made it work on a budget of about $100,000 a year. This was supplied in almost equal measure by five sources: box office, touring, public funding, private foundations and individual contributions. When there was a shortfall, as there always was, the ship was kept afloat by Malina's contributions of her earnings as a now and again movie actress (*Enemies, a Love Story, Awakenings, The Addams Family* and *Household Saints* were filmed during our tenure on Third Street). Certain friends of means, like Peter Ungerleider, Martin Sheen, Al Pacino, and Robin Williams, were also there to help when the going got rough.

Except when on tour, the actors never got paid a living wage. We were too underfunded and too committed to working with a large group of people to be able to pay anybody's rent but the theater's. We were determined to work toward supporting the company, but Judith and I were unable to cover even our own basic expenses with the meager salaries ($200/week) we allowed ourselves, and which the theater was only able to pay some of the time. Our challenge was to keep the theater running, to keep it creating, to make it a magnet for cultural change.

By taking on a space of our own, we freed ourselves from the tyranny of production schedules determined by the availability of other spaces, which was in turn determined by our marketability. Here, instead, we were in a situation where we could afford to do exactly as we pleased, much as Robert Edmond Jones had advised Julian and Judith in the forties.

We would customize the space itself to the needs of each production. Gary Brackett, who had worked with Living Theatre veteran Rain House in Boston, gave of himself unstintingly as technical director, as well as actor, installing equipment, constructing sets, brilliantly enabling our grand ideas to work in the tiny space.

On Third Street we could for the first time set our own opening dates, repertory schedule, and rehearse at times that suited our own needs and desires. These were important advantages for us and we made the fullest use of them, designing every major production as a unique use of the space, placing the audience now on bleachers, then in a circle around us on the floor, or at little cabaret tables, or adrift in a shifting environment. We even managed to tour Europe for months at a time while the remainder of the company continued to keep performances going at Third Street. Further, the space became a real point of reference for the struggling community of East Village/Lower East Side artists and activists. All manner of extratheatrical events took place under The Living Theatre's banner, or rather, behind the brightly elegant yellow neon sign that sculptor Rudi Stern had made for us.

John Farris, a neighborhood *littérateur* and poetic personality did us the great service of taking up residence in the basement dressing room, in exchange for which (plus a small weekly cash sum) he kept watch over the premises, and hosted a regular late-night salon with the wide range of his acquaintances. This was somewhat distressful to Lola Ross, who ran the box office with admirable precision — she felt that Farris' down-and-out style would drive away customers, but eventually she grew to accept his genial presence. Lola was Judith's schoolmate at Piscator's Dramatic Workshop back in the forties, and it was in fact she, along with classmate Robert Hilliard, who first put the idea of creating her own theater into Judith's head way back when. It was touching to see her now actively making the Third Street theater function, both out front as mistress of ticket sales, and onstage, as a member of the acting company.

Despite our accomplishments, it pained me that we were not able to support the company, except for those fleeting months on tour abroad. Among the company, there were only Tom and Carlo who remembered the state of grace in which the company had in the past been supported thanks to Julian's heroic, often desperate, determination to keep everyone housed and fed for all the many years from the company's departure from New York in 1963 through to the end of the Joyce engagement back in New York in 1984. Certainly there was throughout those awesomely adventuresome years no shortage of dead-broke spells and transference anger at Papa Julian and Mama Judith, but somehow, while we kept creating and performing, the company never really had to turn elsewhere for its survival than to the theater itself.

Now, we felt ourselves more spiritually akin to the company that created The Living Theatre during its early years in New York. After all, here we were, back "home," not for a guest season of plays created in Europe, such as the company had presented in 1968–69 and again in 1983–84, but to create new work in a modest rented space much as had happened at the Cherry Lane from 1951–53, at the loft on 100th Street and Broadway from 1954–56, and at The Living Theatre on 14th Street from 1958–63. The company, like the fifties/early sixties company, wasn't living together, nor able to depend on a living wage from the theater work, but like them, we were hungry artists committed to the Living's work even when it wasn't a living. Poetry, now that we were largely anglophone and resettled in the United States, assumed greater importance — our last pre-Third Street productions, Jerome Rothenberg's *Poland/1931*, and Michael McClure's *VKTMS*, were texts by contemporary poets, and we chose a contemporary work of American poetry, Armand Schwerner's *The Tablets*, to open The Living Theatre on Third Street. Judith and Julian had always been moved by Cocteau's choice of *"poter"* as the highest title to which an artist may aspire. We returned the Orpheus drawing which Cocteau had sent the Becks in the fifties to the place it once occupied on Living Theatre programs of that era. Music, too, had renewed importance for us. We worked at Third Street with a series of talented composer/performer/musical directors: Carlo Altomare, Michael Shenker and Patrick Grant, all of whom would integrate a deep understanding of our theater work into their musical contributions. The aura of new beginnings was enchanting.

And we were, in fact, a new beginning. The reimplantation of The Living Theatre into the creative soil of downtown New York would produce a sizable body of unique theatrical invention. We were breathing deeply as we gave ourselves over to the work on Third Street. And if decades had passed since we were the mainstream culture's favorite flavor-of-the-month, that could hardly deter our committed ranks. We felt, we still feel…. Tennyson probably says it best:

> Come, my friends,
> 'Tis not too late to seek a newer world.
> Push off, and sitting well in order smite
> The sounding furrows; for my purpose holds
> To sail beyond the sunset, and the baths
> Of all the western stars, until I die.
> It may be that the gulfs will wash us down;
> It may be we shall touch the Happy Isles,
> And see the great Achilles, whom we knew.
> Though much is taken, much abides; and though
> We are not now that strength which in old days
> Moved earth and heaven, that which we are, we are-
> One equal temper of heroic hearts
> Made weak by time and fate, but strong in will
> To strive, to seek, to find, and not to yield.
>
> (from "Ulysees")

# 1

# THE TABLETS

Armand Schwerner presented Julian, Judith, and myself with a copy of *The Tablets* in Paris, at a dinner at Procope in 1983. This was during the period following our residency at Nantes, where we created Julian's *Archaeology of Sleep*. Jack Lang had promised Julian in writing that he would work with us to find the company a home in Paris and so we sublet an apartment in the rue Oberkampf, at the edge of the Marais and just around the corner from the splendid Cirque d'Hiver. Throughout those long months spent looking at abandoned wineries, historic theaters in disuse like Copeau's Vieux Colombier (where, in 1961, The Living Theatre had first made its impact on Europe, taking prizes at the Théâtre des Nations for William Carlos Williams' *Many Loves* and Jack Gelber's *The Connection*), night clubs like the Bataclàn, and old cinema-theatres on the boulevards like the Max Lander, *The Tablets* was the focus of our reading that season, and all three of us came to know the poems intimately.

Then Julian was called to New York by Francis Ford Coppola to play a gangster in *The Cotton Club*. One of Coppola's financial advisers was Bernie Gersten, whose wife, Cora Cahan, ran the Joyce Theater, a renovated version of the old Elgin revival house that had lately become one of the city's prime dance venues. Bernie and Cora were interested in presenting theater at the Joyce as well, and proposed a six-week, four-play Living Theatre season to inaugurate the project. At the conclusion of that episode, which had provided an occasion for the New York press, led by the young, retro-minded Frank Rich, to label The Living Theatre as "an undistinguished collection of international riff-raff" devoid of artistic merit, Julian suffered a recurrence of colon cancer that proved fatal. Judith inherited the eight rooms on West End Avenue which the Beck family had inhabited since 1939, and determined to stay. We let the Paris plans lapse and began creating plays again in New York, deciding to rebuild a company here and to find a way to have our own space.

And when we found it we decided to open it with *The Tablets*. Because the occasion was The Living Theatre's return to its origins in New York and the Schwerner poems are precisely about a modern attempt to recreate the very origins of civilization. Because we needed to strip away every layer of illusion about what the culture is. The lie of literature, the lie of language. Schwerner's *Tablets* pit the *materia* itself against an outside critical faculty, embodied in the "Scholar/Translator," a man so genuinely, so completely absorbed in considering the process of considering the material — clay fragments which echo and sometimes cite Sumerian sources — that he bounces back and forth between immersion and alienation, much like the battle between modernism and postmodernism itself. Schwerner presents this graphically as a published translation of presumably ancient clay tablets which are rendered in poetic lineation, with assorted dots, dashes, and computer-generated doodads marking sections identified as "missing" or "untranslatable." These translations are presented with glosses and comments by the Scholar/Translator within which he offers his own troubled ruminations about his work, and especially his growing doubts about the knowability of anything. Armand is one of the many modern, often Jewish, artists of a certain age to whom Buddhism has offered the cleanest approach to spiritual consciousness, and for whom spiritual consciousness serves as the cleanest approach to knowledge.

Finally, it is the way Armand uses *The Tablets* to search for the deeper, hidden meaning beneath all apparent meanings that convinced us to launch the next phase of the work with it. Further, *The Tablets* sets in motion a broad range of spiritual expression, both in the "translation" of various pantheistic, animistic ballads and incantations and in the Scholar/Translator's soul-searching remarks.

Dramatic conflict is inherent in *The Tablets*, deriving from the taut, dialectical relationship between the Sumeriana (full-rendered, often in epic meter) and the Scholar/Translator's attempt to present the material to the public while he is continually besieged by the terrors of self-doubt. In three-dimensional theater space, Schwerner's reader becomes The Living Theatre audience brought face-to-face with both the translator and his conceits incarnate.

The tablets themselves, a multifarious collection of voices, blossom into an ensemble of actors who become collectively the nearly lost poetry of the most distant past come to life. By bringing the actors face-to-face with the audience, we flung the poet's imaginings right into the audience's eyes like circus sawdust, and established power over them like a conquering wave of nonviolent Mesopotamian warriors. With *The Tablets* we were able to establish links with the most ancient of myths and at the same time pose the most contemporary of questions: to what degree does our cultural formation, the structure of our language, our gender, our economic class, our past and current emotional life, our feelings about the divine... to what degree do these curvatures of our perceptions distance us from the substance of reality?

The dramatic arena for the metaphysical-philological joust is a triangular playing area surrounded by audience on all three sides. It was through Kandinsky that I had come to grips with the spiritual properties of the triangle, back when we were preparing *The Yellow Methuselah* in Rome in 1982.

Our obtuse triangle had as its longest side the path from the "Temple Gate," or origin point, at the top of the corner stair to the basement dressing room up and

down which the ensemble appears and disappears to a barred gateway to the theater lobby and exit which we designated "Fish-Death Gate." At the triangle's apex
is the domain of the Scholar/Translator, a snowy-white pulpit or "Ivory Tower."
Ilion Troya, who joined the company during its Brazilian sojourn in 1970–71, did
for *The Tablets* what he would do for every subsequent production at Third Street
— design a unique plan for the use of the space and outfit it as an arena for live interaction between actors and audience. *The Tablets* set provided a softly padded
canvas ground cloth painted in terra cotta tones. The vertices of the triangle were
all elevated. Temple Gate rose perhaps four feet above the floor. From that height,
a steep ramp ran downstage into the main playing area and a steep stairway upstage
connected to the basement stairs. The top of the rise was marked by a pair of vertical pylons from which a huge brass gong was suspended. Diagonally opposite
stood Fish-Death Gate, named for Pinitou's plaintive prayer for a sacrificed son, delivered by Tom Walker as he wrestles with the striped barrier-beam stuck between
the inner and outer spaces. The clay-colored floor rose gently toward the barred
passage-point, and then suddenly down to the theater exit. These elevations gave
physical momentum to movements inward into the space, and therefore favored
movements toward the coming together of the ensemble. They also made moving
out from the central playing area an act of audience-directed individuality. Opposite the diagonal extremities, the Scholar/Translator's refuge rose as a three-stepped
platform topped by a lectern and a white-paper canopy spiraling to the ceiling.
From here, the Scholar/Translator would present his material, though again and
again, his fascination with the material would lead him to step down into the midst
of the ensemble of tablets, though time and again the tablets would turn on him
and send him fleeing to the safety of his tower.

A French costume designer, Bénédicte Leclerc, walked unannounced
through the door one day, impressed us with some photos and sketches and was
soon making costume drawings for *The Tablets*. The poems are divided into two
groups, designated by Schwerner as "the emptying" (*kenosis*) and "the filling"
(*pleurosis*) and the play, consequently, was divided into two acts. In Act I, the
Scholar/Translator appears in a dark, vaguely academic three-piece suit embroidered with Schwerner's symbols for "missing" and "untranslatable" while the ensemble of the tablets themselves are wrapped in archaic-looking swatches of
sackcloth and netting revealing much bare skin. For Act II, I suggested that
everyone appear in underwear, to suggest a shift into more intimate territory.
Bénédicte put the ensemble into white briefs, black socks and slippers and added
white button-down shirts embroidered with the textual symbols. After intermission, during which we offered coffee, pastries, and punch in the lobby, the
Scholar/Translator returns to the fray stripped down to a short-legged union suit.

Carlo Altomare, who in the early 1970's had created the music for *The
Money Tower* and a few years later, for *Prometheus at the Winter Palace* (the two
scores provide the theme music for Sheldon Rochlin and Maxine Harris' 1983
Living Theatre documentary, *Signals through the Flames* and are heard again in

Dirk Szuszies 2003 film, *Resist: To be with the Living*), developed a musical score for *The Tablets* which wove through the play like a stream of consciousness given now to lyric pageantry, now to concrete commentary. Repeatedly, the music would open a distance between spectator and material through "interruptory" sounds and then dissolve that distance through melodic enchantment. Carlo, a sensitive actor and director as well as musician, knows how to create choral atmosphere, and instinctively places the sounds at instructively dramatic angles to the proceedings. He and his partner, a heavenly singer called Penta, nested in a corner of the playing space and animated the proceedings with piano, flutes, drums, and slide-whistles.

John Dodd, a master light designer who developed his sexy, expressionist, colorplay style at the Café Cino way back when, had initiated me into the lumino-mysteries a year earlier when he designed the lighting for *Poland/1931*. For *The Tablets*, Johnny threw a galaxy of light on the production, interweaving various chromatic moods with bright-lit, long-shadowed intervals. Proprietor of an enterprise called Fourteenth Street Stage Lighting (headquartered right in the middle of the meat market) he also did us the enormous service of donating to the theater a full set of lighting equipment: projectors, cables, dimmer packs and board.

The process of creation had begun the previous August with a week-long meeting with Armand in the country during which time we traveled through the entire text, tablet by tablet, and I endeavored to pick his brain for every available clue to his intentions. We began with a bang. He seemed profoundly shocked when I suggested transforming the single Scholar/Translator into a team of researchers investigating various aspects of the tablets: linguistic, literary and anthropological. "But you will lose the power of the greatest phenomenon of the universe, the consciousness of the individual!" he cried. Judith settled the matter by asserting that the first theatrical production of the work of a living author ought to be to be dedicated to fulfilling the author's own vision of his work. Seeing the taurine passion blazing in Armand's eyes, I understood for the first time that he is the Scholar/Translator and proposed that he play the role himself. He declined, saying he would prefer someone like Fritz Weaver, denying, moreover, that he felt any personal identification with the Scholar/Translator. I have often found writers to be very touchy at the suggestion that their work may be autobiographical.

Then there was the task of forging a dramatic script out of the poems. As I had learned while adapting Jerome Rothenberg's *Poland/1931*, staging a collection of poems begins with an examination of its literary structure as an analogy to dramatic plot. In Rothenberg's case the narrative element — the story of his parents' journey to America — provided a dramatic center. Schwerner, on the other hand, has created a cycle of poems which is a dialogue between pseudo-archaeological materials and the figure of the Scholar/ Translator, conducted via the juxtaposition of translation and commentary. This oppositional structure is itself a dramatic situation. Some shuffling in the order of the poems was done to maximize the theatrical potential of the rhythmic sequence. The last published poem is placed at the beginning of the play; it is somewhat retrospective in tone and becomes in our version a prologue-like meditation on the part of the Scholar/Translator as he considers the long arc of his labors.

Identifying unique voices, beyond that of the Scholar/Translator, within the many forms of the poetry was the next step in the process of dramatization. The chorus of *Tablets* would often speak, chant, and sing in unison, but just as often, they would speak as individual elements of the ur-world. Characters were created by distinguishing between the panoply of attitudes and styles of utterance in the poetry. Some were given names that appear in the text: Pinitou, a troubled man who has lost a son to a sacrifice and who has woman-problems to boot, Ahanarshi, a spiritual seeker, Inanna, a veritable goddess of the flesh, and Foosh, a force of nature personified. Others took the names of key words or sounds prominent in the parts of the text they would speak: Belàbedies, a melancholy poet, Aw-Aw-Nib-Gi-Gi, a fiery protester, and Prò, a volatile orgiast. Another group was named after images in the poems: Blue Flower, a maiden initiate, and Crystal, a clear-cut celebrant. Still others were called plainly after their special function: The Questioner, The Answerer, The Facilitator, The Priestess.

At the time rehearsals began, I had done little pre-planning of the staging. Day by day, I devised a general outline for each scene/poem. In Act I, Scene 1, for example, the Scholar/Translator is drawn toward the moving juggernaut of the tablets' pulsating collective body, mounts triumphantly, then topples and is nearly torn apart. In Act I, Scene 4, the ensemble approaches the audience individually and recites to them in confessional confidence a text in what Schwerner calls "Crypto-Icelandic." Act I, Scene 8 is entirely wordless (the original poem, Tablet X, is an arrangement of symbols denoting "untranslatable" and "missing"), the Scholar/Translator observing enraptured as the ensemble assumes a series of highly-charged tableaux accompanied by Carlo Altomare's hyper-galactic electronic sounds. In the final scene, Act II, Scene 6, the Scholar/Translator is left alone, but centered, in the midst of his audience, as the ensemble of tablets slowly climbs the walls of the theater space, by means of hidden hand- and foot-holds, until they reach the ceiling and become the very stars suspended above us.

The basics of the choreography were outlined in advance, but as the ensemble developed a working vocabulary of forms of movement specific to the play, more and more of the actions themselves came to be developed spontaneously in rehearsal.

Armand was present at nearly all the rehearsals, continually making discreet but significant contributions to the development of the theatrical work. It was he, in fact, who solved the puzzle of the play's climax. Quite naturally, the poet suggested that the poet's own recorded voice enter the room at that point (the conclusion of Act 2, Scene 5), and be heard with amazement by the Scholar/Translator, endowing key phrases that had gone before with new meaning. During the early rehearsals, Armand gave notes to the actors directly, but some found this troubling and it was soon decided to channel all suggestions through the director.

As neither Armand nor I wanted to play the Scholar/Translator, and Fritz Weaver was out of reach, we decided on George McGrath, who had acted in our production of Michael McClure's *VKTMS: Orestes in scenes* the year before. He brought a feelingful, clear-voiced intensity to the role that suited the Scholar/Translator admirably. McGrath is some years older than the rest of the company, and he is an actor who places characterization as the center of his work, whereas the ensemble members' idea of theater is rooted more in the soil of physicality and choral expression. Thus, a generational difference in acting style between the Scholar/Translator and the ensemble was part of the dramatic equation from the outset. *The Tablets* are outwardly directed, laying hands on the spectators, whispering in their ears, whereas the Scholar/Translator is inwardly focused, obsessed with his own ambiguous relationship to the material.

The ensemble coalesced powerfully around several extremely strong performers. Tom Walker's Pinitou, Sheila Dabney's Inanna, Alan Arenius' Ahanarshi, Michael Saint Clair's Prò, Elena Jandova's Aw-Aw-Nib-Gi-Gi, and Willie Barnes' Foosh were anchor-points around which energy flowed. The novelty of being a company newly working in its own theater was thrilling to all of us and the world we created within those walls reverberated with that special enthusiasm.

*The Tablets* provoked a decidedly positive response among the large audience produced by favorable reviews. We were particularly pleased that it was popular among the neighborhood kids, though it proved less intelligible to the Hispanic locals than to the black residents of the municipal shelter down the block. We talked from time to time of Spanish-language performances (I did myself play the Scholar/Translator in Spanish on tour in Spain), but unfortunately, we never found the right moment. After its initial run, we brought it back the following winter, in repertory with the equally popular *IandI*. During the summer of 1990, we performed *The Tablets* in Germany, Spain, Italy, and Czechoslovakia. The Germans and Italians were enthusiastic, the Spaniards had the newly-discovered Fura dels Baus company at the festival and paid us little heed, and the Czechs, remembering our clandestine performance of *Antigone* under the police state ten years previous, told us, "When you were here before, nothing was possible culturally, so anything that did happen was enormously important. Now, everything is possible and nothing matters." For the European performances, I elected to replace George McGrath as the Scholar/Translator myself, in order to be able to function literally as a translator for the audience, performing the role in Italian in Italy, in German in Germany, in Spanish in Spain, and in English in Czechoslovakia. This level of linguistic geometry was happily appropriate to the play's concerns and placed the figure of the Scholar/Translator in a more intimate rapport with the public. *The Tablets* was the first Living Theatre production to be created in New York and then performed in European theaters since *The Brig* crossed the Atlantic in 1964.

# Excerpts from Judith Malina's Diary
## May 31, 1989

It is Julian's sixty-fourth birthday. And it is the official opening of the new space of The Living Theatre on Third Street. The little house is full. There's Erika Munk and Steve Ben Israel and Pamela Badyk and Mark Amitin helping manage, and Gianfranco Mantegna and Mary Mary and many such friends in the audience. I watch the first half of the performance sitting beside Garrick [Beck].

The play is — like nothing else. Later Armand says to me in the lobby: "It's a real contribution to Poetic Theatre."

The theme is at last crystal clear… it's about study and learning and about the realization that what we are searching for is forever "untranslatable."

Above where Garrick and I sit there is a family of five who came in from the shelter down the street. A father, a mother, and three toddlers. How do they take this scholarly study? And yet, it's about them and their efforts to understand a world fluent in an alien language, caught outside an exclusive literacy, crying out "untranslatable"….

The three little children sit in terrified fascination, listening to the chants, the music, and watching the imposing rituals, the dances, the bodies flowing towards and away.

It's always so swift and it's over. But the enthusiasm and the praise of friends…. I tell them that it's Julian's sixty-fourth birthday and that at Cedar Park [cemetery] this morning the red roses on his grave were in full bloom and we had played a tape of "will you still need me, will you still feed me when I'm sixty-four!" and everyone had joined in the raunchy choruses, singing loud and bawdy to the memory of Julian.

Singing our hearts out, not to be sad, and to open the new Living Theatre in his honor on his birthday, in his absence and in his inspiration.

Hanon has proven himself beyond anyone's doubt. With these words and this wonderful company he has created a life — a world — a new voice.

Fig. 1
*The Tablets:* Tom Walker as Pinitou   *[Photo: Ira Cohen]*

# EXCERPTS FROM A DIALOGUE
## BETWEEN HANON REZNIKOV
## AND ARMAND SCHWERNER

### June and July 1993

*SCHWERNER*: I remember my shocking meeting with you and Judith in your apartment when — I don't know which one of you suggested —
*REZNIKOV*: It was me...
*SCHWERNER*: — eight, or ten, or eleven, or nine, or three Scholar/Translators.
*REZNIKOV*: Yes. I had thought the Scholar/Translator could be transposed into a committee of researchers trying to interpret these Tablets. It seemed to me an interesting notion, but I remember the violence of your reaction to it and I remember how you said with passion "But the individual is the most glorious aspect of creation and...". Well, I thought you were essentially right, although there was this other layer in the conversation that made me answer "Except perhaps for love."

*SCHWERNER*: And I feel all the better for sticking to my ground, because you know, we have now passed beyond "the death of the author." How do you feel about not having had the chance to design a committee of nine?

*REZNIKOV*: Oh, no regrets at all.

*SCHWERNER*: Which doesn't mean that it might not be hazarded in some way.

*REZNIKOV*: No, it's true. But in doing it our way, we emphasized the Tablets themselves; if we had done it the other way, the Scholar/Translator would have been the more dominant presence.

❊ ❊ ❊ ❊ ❊

*SCHWERNER*: When I went to school, and I think even when you went to school, although you're younger than I am, we learned that in the New Criticism a poem is an integral piece, you don't mess with it. When you took your liberties, agreed-upon liberties, with the text of *The Tablets*, did you at various points feel some kind of struggle about juxtapositions or deletions?

*REZNIKOV*: Not as long as I was sure that it was all right with you.

*SCHWERNER*: One of the reasons that it was not difficult for me to agree to your disposing of the text as you chose has to do with the dialogical, going back to a Bakhtinian idea, the dialogical mode of the work. The fictive context within which all of these Tablets exist makes it impossible to know whether in fact the sequences are "correct" or not. Thus, what you have, in addition to commentaries, which are intercalated and invasive on the part of the Scholar/Translator, what you've got is an endless series of sequences which are not totally trustworthy. So you have an ur-text whose very existence is in profound doubt and whose provenance is mysterious. Thus, it makes it possible to see the entire poem, including what is called prose and what is called poetry, as a series of more or less free-floating elements that do or do not suggest a narrative continuity. I think that this complex texture was successfully embodied in the theatrical production. Not such an easy thing to do. Ask any director who's tried to make a play out of some poems. The path is strewn with terrible failures. I've always been interested in the dismal history of attempts to put poetry into theatrical modes.

❊ ❊ ❊ ❊ ❊

*REZNIKOV*: I'm certainly concerned with the audience as an active presence in the theatrical event. I don't know how important the reader is for you as a writer.

*SCHWERNER*: It's very important… whom do I have in mind when I'm writing, that's not such an easy question to answer. One thing that I do think of, is that when I'm composing — which is a word I like better than writing, because I like the sense of com/position, *come* + *ponere* together — anyway, I often do not conceive of or see in my mind's eye or on my mind's screen — I don't see people as potentially reactive audiences. It's as if I'm doing a kind of dance with myself, as if I were my own interlocutor, my own co-dancer, and thus the process doesn't specifically include a visualized other or others as much as an internalized process in which I respond to an abstractive series of movements.

❊ ❊ ❊ ❊ ❊

*SCHWERNER*: Do you want to talk for a minute about the nature of the kind of body-sculpturing positions that you conceived for this?

*REZNIKOV*: These are rendered as tableaux vivants, mysterious signs expressed entirely with body positions accompanied by some extraordinary and key sounds that are created in relation to these positions. And then a series of flashes, of arrangements in various modes. Say two sets of seven people leaning backwards against each other so that their heads interlaced in a sort of zipper effect, while a very deep electronic pulsing tone was heard. Then the lights came up very bright on these static figures in these mysterious relationships and then the whole disappears into darkness. The lights come up again, and this time we see a series of groupings in which one person seems to be receiving a message from some invisible dimension. He or she seems to be transmitting it to lower figures with whom he or she is in direct physical contact, in some kind of poetic, sculptural way.

❊ ❊ ❊ ❊ ❊

*SCHWERNER*: I had a sudden memory while you were talking, about my first meeting with The Living Theatre company and the ominous or implicitly accusing....

*REZNIKOV*: The antagonism was only on the composer's part as I recall —

*SCHWERNER*: Suddenly, there I was in front of the composer-commissar, and what was his name?

*REZNIKOV*: Carlo Altomare.

*SCHWERNER*: Carlo. Whom I got to like very much after that incident.

*REZNIKOV*: And he did a very good job.

*SCHWERNER*: A very good job. But I remember sitting there. It was my first meeting with you and the company and he said — maybe you remember the exact terms — "What are your politics?"

*REZNIKOV*: It was a rather... well, there was this edge of hostility. He was representing a position that said, "here at The Living Theatre we do plays because we think that they're going to further our political goals and we have specific political goals and we'd like to know, if we're going to do your work, where you're coming from politically."

*SCHWERNER*: That was almost as drastic as nine Scholars/Translators. It was an interesting genesis.

[Transcribed by Armand Schwerner]

Fig. 2 *The Tablets*, Company Photo
Bottom: Carlo Altomare, Penta (Leslie Swanson), Tom Walker,
Pat Russell, Laura Nelson; Middle: Elise Synder, Armand Schwerner,
Michael Saint Clair, Jerry Goralnick, Judith Malina, Elena Jandova,
Amber, Lois Kagan Mingus; Top: Gary Brackett, Willie Barnes, Hanon
Reznikov, Alan Arenius, Laura Kolb *[Photo: Living Theatre archive]*

Fig. 3
*The Tablets:* Chorus (Amber, Sheila Dabney and Lois Kagan Mingus
from left to right in foreground) and Scholar/Translator
(George McGrath, in background)  *[Photo: Ira Cohen]*

# THE TABLETS

By
Armand Schwerner
Adapted for the theater by
Hanon Reznikov

The Living Theatre
1989–90 Season
❀

## PROLOGUE
(from Tablet XXVI)

[THE GRAVEYARD OF THE SEA]

SCHOLAR/TRANSLATOR
Clearly I'm the swimming animal, the light song or the dark song

ENSEMBLE
++++++++++++

SCHOLAR/TRANSLATOR
simple...............
when it's hot I'm wet.......

ENSEMBLE
+++++++++++++++++++++++++++++++++++++++++++++++++

SCHOLAR/TRANSLATOR
what happened yesterday? the lettuce drains the sill colored liquids going up
and down inside me.......... tracks.................. without any time

ENSEMBLE
++++++++++++++++++++++++++++
+++++++++++++++++++++++++++++++++++++++

SCHOLAR/TRANSLATOR
untranslatable
nothing, there's nothing after I cut down the frenzied objects in the dance,
nothing to celebrate or hide from — untranslatable
back is back — untranslatable — a phalanx of my teachers'
changing voices
on the clay road and I lift my head up to the perennial sun, hot red stone in a
blue containing — untranslatable — these small getting older thighs matted
like the floor of the woods
with webs and fists of branches keeping their story

ENSEMBLE
++++++++++++++++++++++++++++++++++++++++++++++++

SCHOLAR/TRANSLATOR
letting drop away
their story — untranslatable — ah the ground yesterday
a vast invitation of voices, wet through by flooding,
alive with drone and crawl,
track and shimmer of beings in love
with the hazy dusk of water — untranslatable —
— untranslatable —
— untranslatable —
— untranslatable —
— untranslatable —
— untranslatable —
— hazy


..................................
....................
....................
.................................. hazy.................

**ACT I, SCENE 1**
(from Tablets I & III)

[CEREMONIES AT AN ALTAR]

INANNA
All that's left is pattern.

SCHOLAR/TRANSLATOR
Shoes?

INANNA
All that's left is shoes.

SCHOLAR/TRANSLATOR
Doubtful reconstruction...

INANNA
I rooted about... like a....... sow for her pleasure.

SCHOLAR/TRANSLATOR
This is an atavism: perhaps 'a fetal pig,' is meant, or 'a small pig,' or goddess.'

INANNA
The power for all of us!

SCHOLAR/TRANSLATOR
I made a mistake...

INANNA
the pig of the mistake...

SCHOLAR/TRANSLATOR
'God' may be meant here...

INANNA
war

ENSEMBLE
good-ness....

INANNA
cunt

ENSEMBLE
marvel

INANNA
cunt

ENSEMBLE
bright-yellow

INANNA
bright-ochre

ENSEMBLE
bright-bright-yellow

INANNA
bright-ochre-yellow

ENSEMBLE
bright-yellow-yellow-yellow-ochre-yellow

SCHOLAR/TRANSLATOR
See Halevy-Cohen, *The Prismatic Function in Early Man:*
*A Study in the Imperceptible Gradations*, University Press, 1922–1962

The emptying of yellow...

ENSEMBLE
he calls himself 'with grey horses'
he is 'having fine green oxen'
with purpose +++++++++++++++++++++ in the dream
+++++++++++++++++++++++++++++++++++ of a sharp blade

SCHOLAR/TRANSLATOR
testicles..........................

ENSEMBLE
for the ground
shit upon the.......................
rain upon the................

saliva upon the....................
heart's blood upon the...............

children's strange and beautiful early blood in the........................... from the
old dryness
he is splayed on the........... like a worn-out pig

SCHOLAR/TRANSLATOR
god?

ENSEMBLE
the blood of the four bodies shad/North
the blood of the four bodies cod/East
the blood of the four bodies mackerel/South
the blood of the four bodies tuna/West

do they destroy the ochre, the shad-code
do they eat?
they wait for the fat pig

SCHOLAR/TRANSLATOR
god?

ENSEMBLE
+++++++++++++++++++++++++++++++++++++++++++++

FOOSH
of the great Ones

SCHOLAR/TRANSLATOR
Ones or One? The number is in doubt. Is this the pig, or an incredible
presage of the early Elohim?

ENSEMBLE
let us hold —

PRO
— the long man upside down

ENSEMBLE
let us look —

THE FACILITATOR
— into his mouth... selfish saliva

ENSEMBLE
let us pluck —

CRYSTAL
— for brother tree

ENSEMBLE
let us kiss —

THE QUESTIONER
— the long man, let us carry the long man

ENSEMBLE
let us kiss —

FOOSH
— the long man, let us fondle the long man

ENSEMBLE
let us carry —

THE ANSWERER
— the long man as the ground sucks his drippings

ENSEMBLE
let us bypass —

AHANARSHI
— the wisent on the river-road —

ENSEMBLE
— pintrpnit!
let us avoid —

PRO
— the urus on the river-road —

ENSEMBLE
— pintrpnit!
let us smell —

PINITOU
— the auroch on the river-road —

ENSEMBLE
— pintrpnit!
when the rain comes
let us have rain
let us have rain
let us have rain
let us have — rain
+++++++++++++++++++++++

SCHOLAR/TRANSLATOR
untranslatable

PINITOU
tremble

ENSEMBLE
and also to make the strangers piss in their pants for fear
and to make all the neighbors know of the terrible — that is ours
let them hear about it, let them know
let them tremble like a spear going through the heart and through the back
I need to feel my solid arm, I need to feel my mighty penis
o might, o mighty, o mighty, penis, penis...

PINITOU
o my son at the other edge of fish-death
o my son by the dark river-road I can't reach your fingertips
o my son in the rain your liver will make the barely shoot up
o my son in the rain your eyes will see the way in the wheat
o my son on the happy edge of the emptying, fish-death, pintrpint
o dark dark dark dark

ENSEMBLE
dark dark dark dark dark dark
o dark
you-will-would-might-have-can
let us have rain

## SCENE 2
(from Tablet IV)

### [TWO PLACES AT ONCE]

### SCHOLAR/TRANSLATOR
Most large fragments are the result of horizontal breaks. These tablets, however, are vertically fractured. The edges do not meet in three places. Otherwise, it is a good, tight fit.

### THE QUESTIONER
is the man a bush on fire?

is the man four-legged and with teeth?

is the man a hot woman?

is he mud, of solid mud?

is the man sleeping in a god?

can the man make himself come?
can the woman come on top of the man?
does the man wipe her belly
with sperm?
does the man put good leaves
under his testicles?

does the man put his lips on
the sheep's udder?
does the man put hand and
elbow in his cow's vagina
does he ram his penis into
soft earth?
does he touch his woman's....?

### THE ANSWERER
like one drop of quartz, two cold
onyx beads

like one piece of petrified wood
like one hard-finger-bone, one

moonlight on iron
in the shape of one clay tablet
in frost
like a frog stuff with small
white stones
like a ........ cold onyx beads
....... dead trees
like stories about ice, about
frozen wheat
+++++++ of maggots


in the shape of a clay tablet
in frost
like death in blossoms when....

like the death in petrified wood

like the death in two cold onyx
beads


**SCENE 3**
(from Tablet VI)


[BEYOND THE PALE]


SCHOLAR/TRANSLATOR
Here I have tried to approximate the colloquial tone of the original. Unfortunately we have no information about the identity of the addressee —


PINITOU
I can't come
you have oozed into my +++++++++++++ old Water Dryer
because when I reach the end of my story, I'll still have
all of it to tell in me waiting to explode
like the constipation in a plugged-up man after—


SCHOLAR/TRANSLATOR
untranslatable


PINITOU
Big Mover I still can't come, my woman is unhappy with me

she waits but she's getting +++++++++++++ and madder old Water Dryer you
are fat tree-gum and fungus in my loins
this is not me, o Pa-Pa-the-Flying-Slime, this is not me
I am not what I was
I will call you simple death
Let me blind you Pnou
o Pinitou Pinitou Pinitou —

SCHOLAR/TRANSLATOR

Curious; if this is the surname, or given name, of the speaker, we are faced for
the first time with a particularized man, *this* man, rescued from the prototypi-
cal and generalized 'I' of these Tablets. If it is *this* man, Pinitou, I find myself
deeply moved at this early reality of self; if we have here the name of an unknown deity or peer of the speaker, I am not deeply moved.

PINITOU
— my mouth is full of blood Beautiful

SCHOLAR/TRANSLATOR
Strange?

PINITOU
— Liar
I will call you
simple death, let me blind you Pnou
for Pinitou for Pinitou
who knows me I know me this is not me

SCHOLAR/TRANSLATOR & PINITOU
O my son by the dark river-road —

PINITOU
— river-road I can't touch your fingertips
please let me touch you
and tear your —

SCHOLAR/TRANSLATOR
untranslatable

PINITOU
I will fondle you, I will open you up and eat your +++++++++++

SCHOLAR/TRANSLATOR
missing

PINITOU
knock in breaking +++++++++++++

SCHOLAR/TRANSLATOR
missing

PINITOU
flames Killer of Water ++++++

SCHOLAR/TRANSLATOR
missing section

PINITOU
The One of No Way — unhappy with me
in the world, this place

**SCENE 4**
(from Tablet VII)

[THE CONFESSION]

SCHOLAR/TRANSLATOR
Unfortunately most of the following Tablet cannot be rendered into English.
It has never been recovered. The original, which later disappeared, somehow
passed into the hands of a certain Henrik L., an archeologically gifted Norwe-
gian divine, who inserted Lutheran religious material. How he, working alone
in the semi-darkness of late-19th-century archaeology, managed to make anything at all of the text, which he translated into Crypto-Icelandic, a language
we cannot yet understand, is itself a surpassing wonder.

ENSEMBLE
rötete rötete rötete *p*ropörpe nok pintrpnöte
hraldar gronen panakomen gardu
etaioon pnaupnau gott Jesu Kriste

virtuö er enn eö hvat?
*p*ögn of gat hroiröuk papapa............

SCHOLAR/TRANSLATOR
Faigöar orö

ENSEMBLE
rötete rötete rötete Jesu Kriste sakrifise
*p*orgilson *p*ranodon hvat hvat papa
leggi steypoir pintrpnöte
folklass *p*anns punka hworis
...punka hworis
vituö er enn eö hvat?
festr mun stilna/ok freki rinna

hraldar gronen Jesu Kriste sacrifise*p*ranodon
pögn gardu etaion nok *p*ök
panaknomen proporpe pintrpnote ak Pinitu


vituö er enn eö hvat?
festr mun stilna/ok freki rinna

SCHOLAR/TRANSLATOR
This is the only clear section. Written in Classical Icelandic, it means, "The
chain will break/the wolf will get out."

ENSEMBLE
ok freki ok freki ok freki ok freki ok freki


SCENE 5
(from Tablet V)

PRO
is the man bigger than a fly's wing?
is he much bigger than a fly's wing?
is his hard penis ten times a fly's wing?
is his red penis fifteen times a fly's wing?

ENSEMBLE
what pleasure!
what pleasure!
what pleasure!

SCHOLAR/TRANSLATOR
What pleasure!

AW-AW-NIB-GI-GI
is his mighty penis fifty times a fly's wing?

ENSEMBLE
what pleasure!

HIGH PRIESTESS
does his penis vibrate like a fly's wing?

ENSEMBLE
what terrific pleasure!

CRYSTAL
is his arm four-and-one-half times a strong penis?

AHANARSHI
... a great arm

THE QUESTIONER
is his arm two-hundred-twenty-five times a fly's wing?

THE ANSWERER
... in the shape of petrified wood

FOOSH
does the man touch his body with pleasure?

ENSEMBLE
what pleasure!

BELABEDIES
does she count fly's wings throughout the night?

ENSEMBLE
what pleasure!

INANNA
is her vulva tipped with spring color?

ENSEMBLE
what terrific pleasure!

BLUE FLOWER
does he move behind in her?

ENSEMBLE
let us have rain!

THE FACILITATOR
does she vibrate like the wheel on the axle?

ENSEMBLE
let us have rain!
let us have rain!
let us have rain!

SCHOLAR/TRANSLATOR
what pleasure!

ENSEMBLE
let us call a fly's half-wing *kra*

let us call a fly's half-wing *kra*

PRO
lay a *kra* on this bull's horn
lay another *kra* on this bull's horn

SCHOLAR/TRANSLATOR
let us call a fly's half-wing *kra*

THE QUESTIONER
hold the bull down quiet!

INANNA
let us call the man's red penis *pro*

THE FACILITATOR
lay a *pro* on this cow's vulva

INANNA
let us call the man's red penis *pro*

CRYSTAL
lay another *pro* on this cow's vulva

INANNA
let us call the man's red penis *pro*

THE QUESTIONER
lay another *pro* on this cow's vulva

MUSICIANS
*pro kra kra pro kra kra kra pro*

ENSEMBLE/WOMEN
*kra*

INANNA
what pleasure!

ENSEMBLE/MEN
*pro*

SCHOLAR/TRANSLATOR
what pleasure!

BELABEDIES
let's sacrifice this twig

ENSEMBLE
what pleasure!

THE FACILITATOR
let's sacrifice this great melon

ENSEMBLE
what a pleasure!
let's sacrifice this shank
what a terrific pleasure!

THE ANSWERER
the hand is furious

ENSEMBLE
how will we frighten the strangers now?

PINITOU
the aching head screams

ENSEMBLE
how will they piss in their pants?

AHANARSHI
the sick groin is furious

ENSEMBLE
how will we frighten the strangers now?

++++++++++++++

SCHOLAR/TRANSLATOR
for water

**SCENE 6**
(from Tablet VIII)

[THE BLIND ALLEY]

FOOSH
go into all the places you're frightened of
and forget why you came, like the dead

AHANARSHI
what should I look for?
what should I do? where?
who is my friend? a little stone, a lot of dirt, a terrible headache
and more than enough worry about my grave. Hogs
will swill and shit on me, men
will abuse me
what am I supposed to do then?

FOOSH
the right words wait in the stone
they'll discover themselves as you chip away,
work faster, don't think as long as you want,
like the men who wait

AHANARSHI
what a cold place
this curse better work;
here it is
but what a cold place
to work fast in
I'm getting stiff, this curse
better work:

CRYSTAL
if you step on me
may your leg become green and gangrenous
and may its heavy flow of filth
stop up your eyes forever, may your face
go to crystal, may your meat be glass
in your throat and your fucking
fail. If you lift your arms in grief
may they never come down and you be known
as Idiot Tree and may you never die

PRO
if you pick your nose on my grave
may you be fixed forever in a stupid
attitude, may the children use you
as a jungle gym and turn your muscles to piss,
may you never find a place to sit
and your backbone tire beyond relief,
wherever you stumble around may your heavy feet
squish urus dung and you smell like plague
and you be known
as Fool and Loser and may you never die

THE FACILITATOR
if you throw your garbage on my grave
may its spirit haunt you and sneak into your bed
may your skin become viscous
from the visits of grease, may your woman
become bright with loathing
and sneer at your balls. May your nostrils
be stuffed with the spirit of garbage
and may you be known as Big Nose and Fat Head
and may you never die

FOOSH
whoever drinks in this spirit of Ending
comes at last to these frightening places
and finds rock for his mallet

ANAHARSHI
untranslatabl-

SCHOLAR/TRANSLATOR
The spectator who has followed the course of these Tablets to this point may
find that there is a growing ambiguity in this work of mine, but I'm not sure
where it lies. Some days I do not doubt that the ambiguity is inherent in the
language of the Tablets themselves; at other times I worry myself sick over the
possibility that *I* am the variable giving rise to ambiguities. Do I take advantage of the present unsure state of scholarly expertise? On occasion it almost
seems to me as if I am inventing this sequence and such a fantasy sucks me
into an abyss of almost irretrievable depression, from which only forced and
unpleasurable exercises in linguistic analysis rescue me.

**SCENE 7**
from Tablet IX

[THE DEMONSTRATION]

AW-AW-NIB-GI-GI
I walk when I walk

BLUE FLOWER
when I walk I walk

HIGH PRIESTESS
I walk when I walk, they...
they follow they afflict they follow

SCHOLAR/TRANSLATOR
— with jealousy

AW-AW-NIB-GI-GI
I walk when I walk

SCHOLAR/TRANSLATOR
— with jealousy

BLUE FLOWER
when I walk I walk

SCHOLAR/TRANSLATOR
— with jealousy

HIGH PRIESTESS
I walk when I walk...
they follow they afflict they follow

SCHOLAR/TRANSLATOR
— with jealousy

AW-AW-NIB-GI-GI
when I walk, I walk, I must say I walk when I walk


**SCENE 8**
(from Tablet X)

[THE PANTOMIME OF ECONOMIC RELATIONS]

ENSEMBLE

```
.............................++++++++++++++++++++++++
+++++++++++++++++++++++++++++++++++++++++++++++++++++++
     ++++++++++++++++++++++++++
     ++++++++++++++++++++++++++
     ++++++++++++++++++++++++++
++++++++++.......................@@@@@@@@@@@@@@@
.........++++++++++++.......+++++++++++++++++
++++++++++++..........+++++++.......++++++++++++++++++
     ........................................
.............................@@@@@@@@@@@@@@@@@@@@@@@@
++++++++++++++++++++++++.............+++++++++++++++
          ++++++++++
```

SCHOLAR/TRANSLATOR
the the

## SCENE 9

(from Tablet 11)

[THE CITY SQUARE]

MUSICIAN
whenever I was open I was closed —

SCHOLAR/TRANSLATOR
Who is speaking here?

THE QUESTIONER
where? when you took them with him?

INANNA
she opened her vagina so late it was no prophecy it was —

MUSICIAN
whenever I opened your vagina —

SCHOLAR/TRANSLATOR
Who is the narrator?

AHANARSHI
she was a prophecy no later drainage could make up for

INANNA
and never mind the vats of fresh —

SCHOLAR/TRANSLATOR
Urus-shit? Spermy... frogs? Who is speaking here?

HIGH PRIESTESS
she took them with them for her

PINITOU
where? with him for it?

BLEABEDIES
she opened her +++++++++++++++++++++ and never minded

THE FACILITATOR
she took him splayed from them to cover it —

SCHOLAR/TRANSLATOR
Singular confusion of pronouns here. I do not know who I am when I read
this. How magnificent.

AW-AW-NIB-GI-GI
and cry with the force of testicles

ENSEMBLE
aw-aw-nib-gi-gi

SCHOLAR/TRANSLATOR
This verbal, 'o answering answerer,' operates in the hortatory vocative imper-
ative, an idiosyncratic tense, apparently a mood, but most clearly a real case.
Cognates in the later Semitic (as for instance Square Arabic) assure us that
the term represents nothing less than a scream of despair, released at high
pitch after the solemn incantation of three low notes. Interestingly the scream
leads into the magic barter list, itself maybe a cover for forbidden Utopian
speculations.

AW-AW-NIB-GI-BI
But if you do, give 17 washingstones for 1 cylinder seal in exchange

MUSICIAN
give a beginning —

SCHOLAR/TRANSLATOR
Hair?

MUSICIAN
— in exchange for a wood zag-sal

SCHOLAR/TRANSLATOR
Zag-sal: an eleven-string — 1.5 octave harp. Apparently the start of a barter
ritual ..... a wig for an instrument here?

FOOSH
give a mountain-size platter in exchange for a horde of our people

THE ANSWERER
give a risen stalk, give a giant rye in exchange for...

SCHOLAR/TRANSLATOR
According to Saggs, the lecture was, and still is, responsible 'for the transmission of a great deal of water-borne disease.'

CRYSTAL
give fresh yoghurt in exchange for a horde of our people

PINITOU
give a great netting of fish in exchange for a huger-servant

THE FACILITATOR
giving a milking-stool and a calf in exchange for a thin wormy thigh-bone

PRO
give a bone spoon

BLUE FLOWER
and another bone spoon

BELABEDIES
and another bone spoon

INANNA
and another bone spoon

HIGH PRIESTESS
and another bone spoon

AHANARSHI
in exchange

SCHOLAR/TRANSLATOR
The phrase 'in exchange for' shows every possibility of also meaning 'for the benefit of.'

ENSEMBLE
give a drainage system for the miserable without pattern

SCHOLAR/TRANSLATOR
Shoes? We know that only government buildings in the archaic context had

drainage systems. So this line is of transcendent importance. In it we finally meet, unequivocally, the direct thrust of the first socialist voice in recorded human history. The single voice cries out in early compassion. Who can now easily doubt that the formula 'in exchange for' served as a mask for the writer's anti-hierarchical intent? No contemporary of mine can conceive of the genius and it will be necessary for one man to break through the almost total thought-control of the archaic hierarchies.

ENSEMBLE
in the shadow of fingernail
in the shadow of punctures like steaming vats
and a life, and a life, and a life, and a life, a life, a life... for man


SCENE 10
(from Tablet XII)


[THE FLAME QUESTION]

SCHOLAR/TRANSLATOR
This tablet constitutes an extraordinary find, and an even more extraordinary translation. I present with delight the first musically notated chant in written human history, the Sumerian Hymn on the Creation of Man:

INANNA & FOOSH
and now, what
would you have us do now?
what more do you ask for?

that was the question
at the time of the making of a pair
earth and heaven
and at the time
of our mother Inanna
when she came
— so it went

when earth was laid in its place
and heaven fitted
when straight-line stream and canal ran
when Tigris filled the bed
and Euphrates filled the bed

the god An
and Enlil the god
and Utu the god
and the

god Enki

sat in a high place
and alongside them
the gods Anunnaki of the earth
— so it went

and now
what would you have us do now?
what more do you ask us for?

what's left, what
for us to make?

the two Anunnaki gods of the earth
had a thing to say to the great Enlil:
earth and heaven meet, they say,
at the high place Uzuma
in that high place kill
the craftsman-gods, both of them
and from their blood
make a man and more men

SCHOLAR/TRANSLATOR
For all its hope and spiritual valor, we are in this twentieth century at an end.
It is a mere 5,000 years since, and the story near over.

INANNA & FOOSH
ud an-ki-ta tab-gi-na til-a-ta-es-a
Dingir ama Dinger Inanna-ge e-ne ba-si-sig-e-ne
ud ki-ga-ga-e-de ki-du-du-a-ta
ud gis-ha-har-an-ki-a mun-gi-na-es-a-ba
e pa-ri ~u-si-sa ga-ga-e-de
uzu-mu-a-ki dur-an-ki-ge
Dingir nagar Dingir nagar im-man-tag-en-zen
mu-mud-e-ne nam-lu-galu- mu-mu-e-de

* *INTERMISSION* *

**ACT II, SCENE 1**
(from Tablet XIII)

[THE OBJECT LESSON]

INANNA
this chair

SCHOLAR/TRANSLATOR
this chair

AHANARSHI
this yellow table

PRO
these pots

SCHOLAR/TRANSLATOR
this tablet-clay this...

THE QUESTIONER
lettuce

SCHOLAR/TRANSLATOR
this lettuce
this stone jar

BLUE FOLWER
these blue flowers

SCHOLAR/TRANSLATOR
this silver lioness this...

SCHOLAR/TRANSLATOR & THE ANSWERER
electrum ass on her rein-ring

SCHOLAR/TRANSLATOR
here's my eye

THE FACILITATOR
and here's the great emptiness surrounding the... object

SCHOLAR/TRANSLATOR
hating me
this tablet-clay
hating me
separated from its name

AW-AW-NIB-GI-GI
this stone jar

SCHOLAR/TRANSLATOR
hating me

PINITOU
separated from its name

BELABEDIES
outlining a piece of the air

SCHOLAR/TRANSLATOR
to sliver me through

CRYSTAAL
this piece of blue flower

SCHOLAR/TRANSLATOR
hating me
surrounding myself in anger with me
hating me
the white-green light around the scribe

CRYSTAL
the market-pile

HIGH PRIESTESS
the lettuce

SCHOLAR/TRANSLATOR
hating me in a white-green light separated from its name to sliver me

FOOSH
with ice

SCHOLAR/TRANSLATOR
Psychotic rant, but the author of this Tablet was very likely a "cured"
schizophrenic looking back, intensely directed to assess her past.

INANNA
Last year, I had a woman open to the rain and flood

PRO
Or else a man with breasts shining in a brass light in a room

MUSICIANS
walk-death

ENSEMBLE
walk-death

MUSICIANS
walk-death

ENSEMBLE
walk-death

SCHOLAR/TRANSLATOR
missing —

tablet tablet how do you go
I don't know


**SCENE 2**
(from Tablet XV)


[THE TEMPLE COURT]

INANNA
much, heavily flying, much, heavily flying, much, the vagina musk bleeding
they bring in the wild ass
slow spectrum enormity penis enormity ravage till
much, spectrum, soil tiller, heavily flying and till till vagina musk
they bring in the wild ass
never of when whenever coming coming coming now power ziggeraut tureen
of much, heavily flying enormity ravage penis in sperm mass blue

river god — testicles —
he climbs suspension on my back raw inside lips suspension my teeth
together wild god
nettles nettles sacred bath of sperm and blood bronze in my sleep

SCHOLAR/TRANSLATOR
The next three lines are missing

INANNA
for you, that I turn for you, that I slowly turn for you, high priestess
that you do my body in oil, in glycerin, that you do me, that you slowly do me
that you do me slowly almost not at all, that you are my mouth
that I am your vulva, feather, feather and discover for you — let me open my
thighs for your hands as I do for my own that I do you, that I turn for you,
that I slowly turn for you, high priestess
that you do my body in oil, in glycerin, that you do me, that you slowly do me
that you do me slowly almost not at all, that you are —
that my body becomes a sentence that never stops, driving through air spaces
from one tablet to another, its python power

SCHOLAR/TRANSLATOR
untranslatable

INANNA
unclear, it must be the tips of my own fingers on my cunt lips and your hands
which graze my nipples, looking for what they need, which endear the field of
my closed eyes my closed eyes my nose, the corridor of my ear, my clitoris,
and your wayfaring hands bearing through myself images that are constantly
just escape me because I will not let them win over you
how is it I never knew
this took so much risking

in this small clearing where I rest from us, space inside the field,
emptied of muscle and cries, emptied of muscles and cries
where my money my clothes my blood my lover are violently
plucked away from me
my field sometimes in such pain from thousands of tiny openings
and I wake up unpeopled and startled at such happiness

SCHOLAR/TRANSLATOR
Probably the song of a temple prostitute, priestess of the second caste.

# SCENE 3

(from Tablet XVII)

[THE ASANAS]

AW-AW-NIB-GI-GI
Ahanarshi....... in the Teacher's room........ Ahanarshi ++++++++++ for the
Teacher............ interview
Ahanarshi+++++++++++++++++++++++++++++++++++++++++++++++

SCHOLAR/TRANSLATOR
'Ahanarshi's trip': An archetype of spiritual friendship pervades the text, some
of whose quality arrives at later refinements in Judeo-Christianity.

CRYSTAL
and the vibrations of Ahanarshi's water body were tempest Ahanarshi did a
headstand — to homogenize his fluids, he used the meditation-pillow to prop
himself up on, he sat in the lotus flower...

AHANARSHI
Ahanarshi

CRYSTAL
At the feet of the Teacher

AHANARSHI
Ahanarshi

THE FACILITATOR
By the Teacher, gently by the Teacher.
Ahanarshi wanted to talk, wanted...............................
wanted ++++++++++++++++++++++ but settled; he slid
into himself, turquoise vase,
dust pieces strike him, Ahanarshi, his crystal body
gong........................ sea-wind of the double flutes

BELABEDIES
Ahanarshi sees his heart is a frost-cake, he sees his heart, the smell
of low-tide decay invades his rust nostrils
...........++++++++++++++
He, stiff as a penis, prone on the river belly

sees inside
........................rest++++++++++++++++++++++++++++++++++++++
is it clear is it clear? He says,

AHANARSHI
'Pain, pain'

THE ANSWERER
Ahanarshi says

AHANARSHI
'Pain, pain'

THE ANSWERER
He reenters his activity
he is present
Ahanarshi no longer concentrating now
he hears air circulating in and out of the Teacher
he splinters into a mine
the Teacher says:

SCHOLAR/TRANSLATOR
'We will work together'

AHANARSHI
The Teacher says 'we will work together'

THE ANSWERER
the single mind................. to discover

SCHOLAR/TRANSLATOR
Invent?

AW-AW-NIB-GI-GII
the Teacher

**SCENE 4**
(from Tablet XVIII)

[THE SOURCE OF HEAT]

AHANARSHI
We should always live in the empty sky

PINITOU
this is no dark empty sky
.......... probe mother for the heat source
HOW DOES IT ALL WORK
TEAR IT          GUT HER          GUT THAT ENEMY          DON'T JUST
SIT THERE

HIGH PRIESTESS
o is it dry loam?

ENSEMBLE/WOMEN
dry loam dry loam dry loam
dry dry dry dry dry dry dry dry dry dry dry dry dry dry dry dry
dry loam dry loam dry loam dry loam dry loam
loam loam loam loam loam loam loam loam loam loam loam

PINITOU
my own rust face in the red channel
o my son under this cicatrice earth belly-road I can't touch
fingertips
what is it that gives family? you root in my dream
loam loam nightmare-root boy a
boy goes to school you you ++++++++++++++++++++++++ establish

HIGH PRIESTESS
no loam

ENSEMBLE/WOMEN
no loam no loam no loam no loam no loam...

PINITOU
establish no-loam

SCHOLAR/TRANSLATOR
who are you establishes? a source? sources?
no shoal here no point of arrest

PINITOU
DO IT GET THAT ENEMY DON'T JUST SIT THERE BITE INTO
HER FAT HEART VEIN

DO IT DO IT DRINK WHAT YOU FIND
BLOOD LOAM BLOOD LOAM
HIGH PRIESTESS & ENSEMBLE/WOMEN
o loam o loam loam loam loam loam loam loam

PINITOU
visioning what? dream? no watcher

SCHOLAR/TRANSLATOR
no need to sleep more?

## SCENE 5

(from Tablets XX, XXI, etc.)

[THE LABYRINTH]

INANNA
we have begun to say goodbye to each other.............
and cannot say it finally —the witch Immediacy rides me

SCHOLAR/TRANSLATOR
I take this as an internalization

AHANARSHI
I Ahanarshi the scribe
..... claws move inside my scrotum
the scrapings of idiot compassion for myself

SCHOLAR/TRANSLATOR
The word is abnu-apsu, which usually means 'abyss.'

PINITOU
and you now on the far-side of my life
To a beloved figure disappearing I write in folded tablets

SCHOLAR/TRANSLATOR
An apparent reference to schoolboy tablets, which calls into interesting question the scribe's age at this writing.

BELABEDIES
what is the pain that rises up?

it is.................. it is the pain of the youth
of my life now tainted with spots of age and regret

THE FACILITATOR
the youth of my life to which you'd given yourself
and how is it I could not have seen?

PRO
the teacher and life-changer you loved is now the student of the oppressive-
ness for you that is his singing voice++++++++++

HIGH PRIESTESS
the pain: that every phrase I inscribe
evokes from you yet another distancing from the scribe
so ill at ease in the man

SCHOLAR/TRANSLATOR
I always seem to be too late
for the dancing. This piece of knowledge I've earned
I've earned too dear, o my dear, I
arid and.............. and self-assured before knowing you
arid again after the great
woman-gift of my life. After that
what forgiveness from me
to my life. I'm left with words and no flesh
of your moving spirit to dawn the world.

ENSEMBLE
++++++++++++++++++++++++++++++++++++++++++++++++

SCHOLAR/TRANSLATOR
do I invent you?

PINITOU
o you now on the far side of my life

SCHOLAR/TRANSLATOR
My life, zunnu: also 'rain.'

ENSEMBLE
I have lost...

SCHOLAR/TRANSLATOR
we have begun to say goodbye to each other and cannot say it finally
my untranslatable torsion of anger.................
we..............I .................

ENSEMBLE

++++++++++++++

THE ANSWERER
and how I loved your face

SCHOLAR/TRANSLATOR
'in the half-light' I said

THE QUESTIONER
'yes in the half-dark' you said

THE FACILITATOR
and how many times then a staggered inner-halting for me

SCHOLAR/TRANSLATOR
the word is nakru-salmu, a hostile image.

CRYSTAL
up against your self-contempt I felt as +++++++++++++++++

HIGH PRIESTESS
I write these forms to you whom I have lost

BELABEDIES
my scribe-companions dismissible +++++++++++++++++++++++++

SCHOLAR/TRANSLATOR
and I track with surprise

ENSEMBLE

++++++++++++++++++++++++

## 2

# TUMULT, OR CLEARING THE STREETS

Having opened our indoor space in the late spring, we determined to bring our theater out into the streets come summer. In the preceding year, there had been riots in Tompkins Square Park and a far deadlier confrontation in Tienanmen Square. The common issue was the public's right to use public spaces. We developed a play on this theme and called it *Tumult, or Clearing the Streets*.

We recruited a cast composed of both Living Theatre actors and local people. There were two local children (Cyrus, son of our own Mary Mary and Carlo Altomare) and Melissare Liriano (a charmer from the project on Avenue D), an elementary school teacher from Brooklyn named David J. Feldman, some adventurous Lower East Side artist-activists (Bob Paton, Carmen Waldorf, Denise Gumora, Exavier Wardlaw Muhammad, Initia, Scott Walsh, and Vera Beren). and an intern from Haverford College (Lane Savadove). The Living Theatre actors performing were Alan Arenius, Alexander Van Dam, Gary Brackett, Mary Mary, Michael Saint Clair, and myself.

We approached the creation of the play through group discussions and ensemble exercises, after which I drew up a scenario based on our dialogue and experiments. The plan which emerged was to present each scene of the play in a different location in the same neighborhood, connecting the sites with processions that would carry the audience along with us.

Then, in the play's final scene, we set up a symbolic tent in the form of a maypole with streamers. We gathered the spectators in with us under this suggestion of shelter, rehearsing and then performing with them a choral piece adapted from Alvin Curran's score for *The Yellow Methuselah*.

The performances we gave in parks seemed less effective that those that we gave in streets and vacant lots. The sight of our red, orange, and yellow-clad actors moving theatrically across green lawns was too prettily entertaining to focus the audience's attention on political issues. In the peculiar East Village crucible called Tompkins Square Park, however, participation was at a maximum. The memory of the recent police violence was still fresh. When Mary Mary and I gave the final ultimatum to the sheltering crowd, "You have ten seconds to leave the premises," the rising chorus of protest was fiercely passionate and transformed the play into a true *pièce de résistance*.

Fig. 4, *Tumult*: Street scene    *[Photo: Judith Malina]*

# TUMULT, OR CLEARING THE STREETS

A collective creation of

THE LIVING THEATRE

Summer, 1989


## SUBSECTOR 1 — GATHERING


HE-SHAMAN

Attention. Attention. This is the public sector. Welcome. This is the public sector. Welcome.

SHE-SHAMAN

The time is now four-thirty, exactly.

[ENSEMBLE daily life actions]

HE-SHAMAN

Attention. Attention. This is the public sector, subsector 1. All activities are subject to regulation. All activities are subject to regulation.

SHE-SHAMAN

The time is now four-thirty, exactly.

[ENSEMBLE fear retreat]

ENSEMBLE

Im-pa-tient-ly the peo-ple of New York sit in their fi-re gut-ted hou-ses rot-ting a-way

They earn their bread in canyons
and the smoke chokes them o-ver each sea-son
And the wo-men la-bor dou-ble, wor-king for life at home and in the canyons
And al-ways the end of the world be-ckons to them

SHE-SHAMAN
The time is 4:06, exactly.

ENSEMBLE
But not un-til a-go-ny comes, plun-ging them in-to de-spair, in bon-dage to
debt and to death

Will they rise up and throw off their op-pres-sors

For there is a last straw for them, and then the blind sleep, full of moa-ning
with pre-hi-sto-ric ex-haus-tion, comes to an end.

SHE-SHAMAN
The time is 4:07, exactly.

VOICES FROM ENSEMBLE
Slowly and swiftly...
The moons wax and wane...
Unevenly...
And all the while, evil is growing...
And now, the last light...
Falls on the last root of Authority's power...

[ENSEMBLE begins slow-motion fall]
And when the rich fall...
And when their armed guards fall...
And when property falls...
Then... then... then... then...
Rise... rise... rise... rise...
Up.... up.... up.... up....
Many... many... many... many...

SHE-SHAMAN
The time is now four-thirty, exactly.

[ENSEMBLE approaches audience, begins discussion of Basic
Human Needs]

HE-SHAMAN
Attention. Attention. The subsector is now closed. This subsector is now
closed. Proceed to subsector 2. Proceed to subsector 2.

ENSEMBLE
Basic... Human... Needs...

SHE-SHAMAN
Clear the area immediately. You have exactly five seconds. Five.

HE-SHAMAN
Four.

SHE-SHAMAN
Three.

HE-SHAMAN
Two.

SHE-WOMAN
One.

[HORN — PROCESSION IN SEARCH OF DAILY BREAD]

GARY
Hunger rises up today
but I can't eat if I can't pay

MELISSA
No puedo comparar la comida que necessito
I can't buy the food I would like to eat

VERA
It is not offered to all —
they must be remembered
through our days of delight

SCOTT

DAVE
But now we must live, and eat to live, live beyond shame,
we become the streets we forage to live

INITA

EXAVIER
On the blood of the poor and impoverished masses
we are lords of famine and disgrace

DENISE
Searching for entities that will nurture
our bodies, our souls, our lives

LANE

CARMEN
And with *our* bodies and souls, I mean all people
of the earth, not one person shall starve anymore

## SUBSECTOR 2 — GETTING FOOD

SHE-SHAMAN
The time is now — — — —, exactly.

[ENSEMBLE hunting and farming etudes]

SHE-SHAMAN
The human population of the United States is 243 million.

HE-SHAMAN
The number of human beings who could be fed by the grain and soybeans
eaten by U.S. livestock is 1 billion 300 million.

SHE-SHAMAN
The sacred food of Native Americans is corn.

HE-SHAMAN
The percentage of corn grown in the United States which is eaten by human
beings is 20%.

SHE-SHAMAN
The percentage of corn grown in the United States which is eaten by livestock
is 80%.

HE-SHAMAN

The percentage of carbohydrate wasted by cycling grain through livestock is 99%.


[HUNTERS SHOOT, TIME DACTYL]


SHE-SHAMAN

The frequency of childhood death by starvation
is one child every two seconds.


HE-SHAMAN

The frequency of heart attacks in the United States
is one attack every 25 seconds.


SHE-SHAMAN

The most common cause of death in the United States is heart attack.


HE-SHAMAN

The risk of death from heart attack of the average American is 50%.


SHE-SHAMAN

The risk of death from heart attack of the average American vegetarian is 4%.


HE-SHAMAN

The occupation with the highest employee rate of injury in the United States
is that of slaughterhouse worker.


[HUNTERS SHOOT, TIME DACTYL]


SHE-SHAMAN

The percentage of resources consumed in the United States to produce the
current meat-centered diet is one third.


SHE-SHAMAN

The percentage of resources consumed in the United States to produce a vegetarian diet is 2%.


HE-SHAMAN

The amount of potatoes that can be grown on one acre of land is 20 thousand
pounds.

SHE-SHAMAN
The amount of beef that can be produced on one acre of land is 165 pounds.

HE-SHAMAN
The number of vegetarians who can be fed on the amount of land needed to
feed one person consuming meat is 20.

SHE-SHAMAN
The number of people who will starve to death this year is 60 million.

[ENSEMBLE choral sound, HORN]

ENSEMBLE
Basic... human... needs...

[ENSEMBLE audience discussion]

HE-SHAMAN
Attention. Attention. This subsector has been declared toxic. This subsector
has been declared toxic. Proceed to subsector 3. Proceed to subsector 3.

SHE-SHAMAN
Clear the area immediately. You have exactly five seconds. Five.

HE-SHAMAN
Four.

SHE-SHAMAN
Three.

HE-SHAMAN
Two.

SHE-SHAMAN
One.

[HORN — PROCESSION IN SEARCH OF A HELATHY ENVIRON-
MENT]

EXAVIER
The air burns my eyes, the rain burns my skin
the food is a sickness, the joy of earth is dead

DENISE
We don't have to do anything but *stop*
and the earth has the power to heal itself

CYRUS
But do we?
let's give ourselves a chance

MELISSA
To breathe freely in our world
and to be free of everything

INITIA
We need to breathe clean life
basic needs, our survival, our future

VERA
Our filthy water spreading constantly
ocean life continually stopping

SCOTT
Our hearts, submerged, resurface in this barrenness
insanity, pain, unforgivingness: only because
the connection was broken

LANE
We can only tell stories of wading in streams,
only read about springs, and fields, and emptiness

DAVE
Dead is the living sea in which I frolicked as a child
the biting air now hangs heavy with poison

GARY
But we can change that if we want
Let's stop this madness before it stops us

CARMEN
But still we shit into the toilet each day
and flush it down into the ocean

## SUBSECTOR 3 — STAYING HEALTHY

### [HORN — PLAGUE]

SHE-SHAMAN
The human race added more than 20 billion tons of carbon dioxide
to the atmosphere through fossil fuel consumption in 1988.

HE-SHAMAN
The United States produces each year more than 18 tons of carbon dioxide
for each man, woman, and child.

SHE-SHAMAN
It is the increasing concentrations of carbon dioxide in the atmosphere that is
leading inexorably to catastrophic global warming.

HE-SHAMAN
Ozone depletion caused by the industrial release of chlorofluorocarbons
is depleting the ozone layer.

SHE-SHAMAN
It is because of the depletion of the ozone layer that it is no longer possible for
human beings to be exposed to direct sunlight for more than a few minutes
without risking skin cancer.

HE-SHAMAN
Even if chlorofluorocarbons are phased out by the end of the century,
the destruction of the Earth's ozone layer will continue for decades.

SHE-SHAMAN
As carbon-dioxide levels have risen, global temperatures have crept upward
by about one degree Fahrenheit over the past 100 years. Climatologists pre-
dict a rise of between 3 and 9 degrees over the next 60 years. This may sound
small, but the greatest temperature changes in history, the changes from the
ice ages to the warmest periods, have never been more than 7 degrees over
*thousands* of years.

HE-SHAMAN
Fifty years from today, the polar ice cap will have melted, with the result that
vast coastal areas, including much of New York City, will be underwater.

SHE-SHAMAN
Forty years from today, at current consumption rates, the world's reserves of
oil will be exhausted.

HE-SHAMAN
Thirty years from today, environmentally caused cancer is likely to be the
leading cause of death in the world.

SHE-SHAMAN
Twenty years from today, because of global warming, the change in the earth's
temperature will be as great as the change that brought on the last ice age.

HE-SHAMAN
Ten years from today, the world's population will more than triple in size to
about 6 billion people. Most of the earth's nations will not be able to feed
themselves.

SHE-SHAMAN
One year from today, at present rates, about 20 million hectares of tropical
rainforest will be leveled and burned. This will increase the carbon dioxide
content of the atmosphere enough to create the so-called, "greenhouse effect."

HE-SHAMAN
Today, [date], despite the availability of resources, 40,000 children died of
hunger.

VOICES FROM ENSEMBLE
(Canto of the Dead)
What time is it?
There is no time.
What happened?
What happened?
Nothing happened.
Nothing happened.
Nothing happens.
Death is the end
of time.
of time.
Death is the nothing.
Nothing.
Death is no time.
No time.
No marvelous music.

Music.
No tone.
No star.
No pulsar.
Pulsar.
No lotus death.
The incomprehensible.
How did it happen?
Who has denied it?
Who dies?
Dies?
No one dies.
Dies.
No one.
No one
dies.
Dies.
Everyone every
one.
Every one
is killed.
Is killed.
Death is
is
a catalogue
a catalogue
of murder.
Death.

What time is it?
there is no time.
What happened?
Nothing happened.
Nothing happened. Nothing happens.
Death is the end
of time.
Of time.
Death is the nothing.
Nothing.
No speech.
No time.
No marvelous music.
Music.

No tone.
No star.
No pulsar.
Pulsar.
No lotus death.
The incomprehensible.
Who has denied it?
Who dies?
Dies.
No one.
No one
dies.
dies.
Everyone every
one.
Every one
is killed.
Is killed.
Death is
is
a catalogue
a catalogue
of murder.
Death.

[ENSEMBLE rolls out of body pile, begins audience discussion]

HE-SHAMAN
Attention. Attention. This subsector is now closed. This subsector is now closed. Proceed to subsector 4. Proceed to subsector 4.

SHE-SHAMAN
Clear the area immediately. You have exactly 5 seconds. 5

HE-SHAMAN
4

SHE-SHAMAN
3

HE-SHAMAN
2

SHE-SHAMAN
1

[HORN — PROCESSION IN SEARCH OF REFUGE]

DENISE
Shall we stop and examine the social dynamics at play?

GARY
Because any hate only furthers more hate —
so free your mind and let's have this free place

CARMEN
Dream, dream, dream about better life and love
and the theatre is my refuge where I share my
dreams with you

DAVE
Away from cars and trucks, horns and blasts trapped
in traffic they grind continually into my skull

BOB

———————————————

EXAVIER
Am I free to be black and not the black thing you hate
am I free to be a man and not the men that you hate?

INITIA
I will not rest until I am recognized, when my family,
my friends, my lovers have nothing to fear

MELISSA
Then we can stand as one
Ahora podemos pararnos juntos

SCOTT

———————————————

VERA
But you throw them in my face — and that I've no right
to stop this torture of our souls

## SUBSECTOR 4 — FINDING REFUGE

[PROCESSION 3, VERA: "...our souls," ACTION, HORN]

### HE-SHAMAN
Attention. Attention. This is the public sector, subsector 4. This is the public sector, subsector 4.

[ENSEMBLE constructs shelter]

### SHE-SHAMAN
All unauthorized activity is forbidden. All unauthorized activity is forbidden.

### HE-SHAMAN
It is against the law to construct shelter in the public sector. It is against the law to construct shelter in the public shelter.

[ENSEMBLE — AUDIENCE music workshop]

### SHE-SHAMAN
Clear this subsector immediately. Clear this subsector immediately. You have exactly five minutes. Five minutes.

### HE-SHAMAN
Four minutes and forty-five seconds. Four minutes and forty-five seconds.

### SHE-SHAMAN
Four minutes and thirty seconds. Four minutes and thirty seconds.

### HE-SHAMAN
Four minutes and fifteen seconds. Four minutes and fifteen seconds.

### SHE-SHAMAN
Four minutes exactly. Four minutes exactly.

### HE-SHAMAN
What time is it in Tiananmen Square? What time is it in Tiananmen Square?

### SHE-SHAMAN
Three minutes and forty-five seconds. Three minutes and forty-five seconds.

HE-SHAMAN

Three minutes and thirty seconds. Three minutes and thirty seconds.

SHE-SHAMAN

Three minutes and fifteen seconds. Three minutes and fifteen seconds.

HE-SHAMAN

Three minutes exactly. Three minutes exactly.

SHE-SHAMAN

What time is it in Tompkins Square? What time is it in Tompkins Square?

HE-SHAMAN

Two minutes and forty-five seconds. Two minutes and forty-five seconds.

SHE-SHAMAN

Two minutes and thirty seconds. Two minutes and thirty seconds.

HE-SHAMAN

Two minutes and fifteen seconds. Two minutes and fifteen seconds.

Fig. 5 *Tumult*: Prospect Park, Brooklyn   *[Photo: Judith Malina]*

SHE-SHAMAN
Two minutes exactly. Two minutes exactly.

HE-SHAMAN
What happens in Tiananmen Square? What happens in Tompkins Square?

SHE-SHAMAN
One minute and forty-five seconds. One minute and forty-five seconds.

HE-SHAMAN
One minute and thirty seconds. One minute and thirty seconds.

SHE-SHAMAN
One minute and fifteen seconds. One minute and fifteen seconds.

HE-SHAMAN
One minute exactly. One minute exactly.

[ENSEMBLE brings audience under tent]

SHE-SHAMAN
How far is Tompkins Square from Tiananmen Square? How far is Tompkins
Square from Tiananmen Square?

HE-SHAMAN
Forty-five seconds. Forty-five seconds.

SHE-SHAMAN
Thirty seconds. Thirty seconds.

HE-SHAMAN
Fifteen seconds. Fifteen seconds.

[SHAMANS circle shelter]

SHE-SHAMAN
Ten.

HE-SHAMAN
Nine.

SHE-SHAMAN
Eight.

HE-SHAMAN
Seven.

SHE-SHAMAN
Six.

HE-SHAMAN
Five.

SHE-SHAMAN
Four.

HE-SHAMAN
Three.

SHE-SHAMAN
Two.

HE-SHAMAN
One.

SHE-SHAMAN & HE-SHAMAN
Zero.

[CREATION CHORALE]

VOICES FROM THE ENSEMBLE
Are we free?

Not yet.

# 3

# *IandI*

I asked Judith to say something about her staging of *IandI*. This is what she wrote in response:

> The first time I saw the 3rd St. space, Valeska Gert's
> "Beggar Bar," the Village dive where I worked as a
> hat-check girl and occasional singer just before I met
> Julian in the early 1940's, came to mind. Valeska had
> recreated much of the feeling of pre-Nazi Weimar activity
> in that basement: the compressed expressionism,
> the pre-Beat dissoluteness, the world of
> avant-garde cinema, Brecht, Artaud & Mayakovsky
> (who had been her lover), Gert's idea that she invented
> *Unregelmäsigkeit* — all squeezed into that little
> room. Similarly, in *IandI*, I tried to compress an
> enormous amount: film, Brecht, performance artists
> on little platforms (the Ritz Brothers, Faust, and
> Mephisto) — many little stages...All Germans are in
> love with the Faust theme, the simplistic duality of
> god and the devil — all plays are this struggle for
> them — our little black room, like Valeska's — a
> cafe/brothel in which you're cheated out of your
> money — $5 for a coke when you're sweating like
> hell — making the audience feel like Johns... I imagine
> Else Lasker-Schüler like Valeska: a
> flamboyantly crazy, impossible, Weimar figure.
> Lasker-Schüler was part of the equivalent of the Beat
> movement, drawing together the gutter and the highest
> intellectual tradition. And so I staged *IandI* as cabaret
> theater, except for the death-of-the-poet scene which
> is rightly Reinhardtian and climaxes in the sort of romantic,
> audience-pleasing "ahh... effect" which Thomas Mann puts
> down so skillfully in his *Doctor Faustus*.

Fig. 6: *Ian∂I*: Jerry Goralnick
*[Photo: Ira Cohen]*

*Iand̄I* came to our attention when Malina spoke at a conference on translation at Barnard College. There, Beate Bennett, who had been working on various theater projects while teaching public school in New York, presented her translation of the play to Judith and proposed that The Living Theatre attempt it. Else Lasker-Schüler was a highly regarded poet in Weimar Germany who took refuge in Palestine during the Hitler regime and there composed this extraordinary version of the Faust story in which the doctor and his tempter are but two halves of the divided self, whose desperate, misguided conflict erupts into the Nazi disaster.

The play had long been suppressed by the author's heirs, who feared that the work was not of the same quality as her poetry. Or perhaps it was simply because much of the play's language is coarse and the very idea of portraying the Nazis as comical protégés of a Mephisto beloved by Faust was difficult to swallow in postwar Germany. It had finally been produced once or twice there, and was received with tepid, somewhat academic curiosity. The prospect of presenting a work in which the conflict between good and evil is set in the twentieth-century political world and is nonetheless portrayed as rooted in the consciousness of the conflicted individual was a powerful inducement to Judith and The Living Theatre. Moreover, the play was a rare opportunity to speak from a Jewish point of view, both politically, in terms of the Nazis, and theologically, since as the play questions the terms of the traditional Christian division between the Devil and God. *Iand̄I* takes place in Hell but ends in a direct ascent to Heaven by both Faust *and* Mephisto.

The room was laid out in a multi-stage cabaret style elaborated by Judith and Ilion Troya. The audience was seated on padded reinforced milk crates covered with colorfully figured painted canvases abandoned in the street by a local artist. The seats were gathered about tiny round tables topped with sputtering red candles. Between choruses, an ensemble of eight or more horned, scantily-clad "Devils" worked the house, offering Coca-Cola and Devil Dogs at the fiendish price of $5.

Set at an angle slicing off one corner of the space, a tall bridge-like platform atop scaffolding provided the contemplative realm of Faust and Mephisto. High against the wall diagonally opposite hung a semicircular platform where the three Ritz Brothers, repeatedly transforming into the Nazi hierarchy (Judith's idea, not Else's), performed tightly choreographed vaudeville routines. East Village experimental filmmakers Bradley Eros and Jeannie Liotta contributed a mélange of Ritz Brothers clips and battle maps of Europe in flames, projected on a screen behind the trio.

The god Baal sat upon a throne halfway up the rear wall. Nearby, Martha Schwerdlein's kitchen rose above a trap door to the theater basement, into whose depths Joseph Goebbels slid down a rope suspended from the ceiling. And in the lyrical fifth act, the death of The Poet was staged in the lobby, beyond the arched theater entrance, where white curtains were lowered enclosing an oasis of potted trees around a heavenly white platform that seemed a vast garden come from nowhere. The sudden appearance near the close of the play of this previously non-existent playing area was a bona fide *coup de théâtre* that took the audience quite by surprise.

Fig. 7 — *I and I*: Alan Arenius and Elena Jandova
*[Photo: Ira Cohen]*

The acting was particularly strong and showed the coalescing Third Street company to great advantage. Sheila Dabney's portrait of The Poet was drawn with temperament, pride, and sorrow. When Judith Malina later stepped into the role, The Poet became more specifically an image of Lasker-Schüler herself, a woman who had helped shape German culture now considering from distant Jerusalem her homeland's collapse into violence. Michael Saint Clair created a playfully powerful Mephisto in black leather hot pants and golden horns twisting through his dreadlocks, tormenting a depthful, brooding Tom Walker as Faust into desperation and at the last, into transcendence. Elena Jandova brought the coarse lustfulness of Martha Schwerdlein into instructive contrast with the purity of her apparition to Faust as Marguerite. Rain House was a supernatural Scarecrow and Lois Kagan Mingus a strong-willed Editor Swet. Jerry Goralnick contributed a memorable trilogy of performances, first as anti-Nazi martyr Heschel Grynspan, who is stoned by the mob while suspended upside down naked in an open cage careening through the house, secondly, and yet more memorably as Hitler himself, a superbly executed number in which he screams like a German-accented lunatic, and finally as King David singing a peaceful song as he plays his harp.

Beate Bennett was present throughout the project both as translator and as dramaturge, a rarity for us and highly valuable in terms of making accessible to the actors the whole complex panoply of literary and historical points of reference. Carlo Altomare created a wonderfully rhythmic score that kept the text-heavy play moving jauntily along, punctuated by wonderfully singable tunes in the Weimar spirit, including a version of Grieg's "I Love You" which the Poet orders the piano player, known to her as Gin Charlie (played, naturally, by Carlo himself) to play for her and which returned as an unabashedly schmaltzy reprise sung by the whole cast during the curtain calls. And a violin solo played with mad abandon and considerable skill by Philip Brehse.

With *IandI*, the second major production in the Third Street space, we made clear that our use of the room, already broadly unconventional with *The Tablets*, was going to be unique for each play.

The situation of the audience, seated at cabaret tables surrounded by hellfire, was fundamental to their experiencing alongside Faust the torments within and without. Lasker-Schüler was after that, and Malina brought it home.

Michael Merschmeier, visiting from Berlin, wrote in *Theater Heute* that our *IandI*, despite its fundamental roughness, creates in our little backroom a theater more real and creatively alive than any of the well-subsidized stages of Germany. The following summer, we brought the production to Berlin and it won the city's heart. We worried that it was because we enabled the German public to laugh at the Nazis as silly clowns, as only Americans would dare portray them.

2 DEVILS WHEEL IN THE
GREENSPAN CONTRAPTION

" NOE TO THE RACE..."
STONING OF GREENSPAN
BY NAZIS + DEVILS

LAVA FLOWS
NAZIS DROWN
GÖRING STRUGGLES

PUNCTUATED BY GÖRINGS BLUBBERING CRIES

Fig. 8
*IanƏI*: two of Judith Malina's staging sketches

# EXCERPTS FROM JUDITH MALINA'S DIARY

August 13, 1989

We had a really good rehearsal of the fourth act... the technical madness of the lava flow and the marching Nazis is far from solved... but the play goes on around these events.

The play looks very different than it reads... it's funnier, and oddly, simpler.

I enjoy the rehearsals... sometimes Sheila Dabney, Carlo Altomare, or Mary Ann Brownlee [assistant director] take over and add some glittering moments.

August 23, 1989

Run-through a victory! Shelia is incredible. She's been absent for a few days because of her recent eviction notice.... She returns with a character named Else Lasker-Schüler.... She's immersed herself in the biography, in the poetry, and suddenly, at the start of the run-through, there's this old Jewish poet where there was a young black actress... her eyes, her face, her skin tightens around the cheekbones and there's the old lady... and the poetry is here....

September 20, 1989

God help us! It's pouring rain. The theatre floods. Opening night madness, what if it pours down on the audience, will we send them home? Cancel? Give money back? The last minute madness is upon us — I get into the work of painting flat black all over.

Garrick returns from the West. He pitches in instantly, affixing the lobby lights with Hanon....

Ten minutes before the play, I wash off the black paint, dress up and run down into the wet basement for some last minute ideas and pep talk....

The water is still pouring out of the walls and the actors walk on planks set above the flooded floor....

I sit in my usual place. I do that: get stuck with "my" place in the rehearsal period and then refuse to give it up at performance time.... Don Bruckner from *The New York Times* comes and Erika Munk from the *Village Voice*, and Hanon tells me to seat her further back, but I thought I'd seat her in front of the poet. Then she never turned her head to look at Shelia and the whole performance I fret senselessly that she's not looking in the appropriate direction.

The play is splendid. Still, I feel that it doesn't quite communicate on this night as at the last two previews. It's open and the opening is over. Sense of relief....

Fig. 9

*Ian∂I*: Tom Walker, Sheila Dabney, Michael Saint Clair   *[Photo: Ira Cohen]*

# *IandI* on Avenue C
## Beate Hein Bennett

"Sie stricken ihr Leben."
— Else Lasker-Schüler

Sometimes a rare coincidence becomes the source of an even rarer inspiration. The Living Theatre's production of *IandI* by Else Lasker-Schüler was the culmination of a series of rare coincidences and remarkable encounters, in a way symptomatic (and symbolic) of our century and our city — a century of displacements, exile, chance encounters, and renaissance. It was the result of a personal journey as well, or perhaps the intersection of several personal journeys. The journey of *IandI* from Jerusalem to "Alphabet City," the collaboration of a German "war child" and a Jewish rebel on Loisada Avenue (a/k/aAvenue C) — Else Lasker-Schüler would have liked that: The work of three displaced women in the midst of a displaced community. We knit our lives with many skeins.

Else Lasker-Schüler was one of the most extravagant and eccentric figures on the German literary scene between 1904 and 1933 when she, as a Jew (and a "degenerate" artist), had to flee Nazi Germany. In 1939 she settled into a kind of exile in Palestine. During her years in Germany, she not only wrote, she performed and lived poetry; she became a poem, as colorful as her images, as erotic as her metaphors, as forceful as her multiple male personas — Jussuf of Thebes, Tino of Baghdad — and as madly playful as her nonsense rhymes. In Palestine, because of her eccentric and exotic behavior and dress, her politics, and her art, she suffered from ridicule, isolation, and self-doubt. As a young girl growing up in Germany after World War II, I loved her when I read her work and looked at the pictures of this exotic, darkly beautiful, androgynous woman with eyes like black holes. In my fantasy, she represented the tragically lost, intimate part of Germany. In fact, she had been deliberately "lost," because the teachers never told us she was Jewish.

She was presented simply as a German poet who had died in 1945. But her poetry and those eyes told me another story. In 1985 I moved to New York. I brought with me my first draft of a translation of the play, *IandI*, and archival research materials from the final years of Else Lasker-Schüler's life in Jerusalem. I first came across a description of a premiere of the play and its publication in Germany in 1981, which had aroused my interest as a dramaturge and reawakened my desire to delve into the Lasker-Schüler story. In 1983 I spent a month in Jerusalem in the National Library sifting through the Else Lasker-Schüler archive and discovering the bits and pieces of a lost soul. Lasker-Schüler had lived in a tiny room in Jerusalem in the shadow of the ancient Judean hills. She was estranged from contemporary Judaism; she continued to speak and write in German, the publicly despised language of the cauldron from which she had barely escaped. On my daily walks through the ancient city, I heard Hebrew and Arabic spoken, sometimes German; my thoughts were in German, sometimes English — and a feeling of displacement overwhelmed me. It is the sense of being simultaneously alienated by the familiar and acutely close to the foreign that haunts those of us, who, like me and Lasker-Schüler, have left the place of our roots and mother tongue and settled into a strange landscape and an adopted language. In November 1985, I am sitting in a room at Barnard College, attending a conference on translation. Judith

Fig. 10
*Ian∂I*: (clockwise from upper left: Ilion Troya, Joanie Fritz Zosike, Gary Brackett, Alan Arenius, Laura Kolb) *[Photo: Ira Cohen]*

Malina is scheduled to speak. I know of her, of course, but I had never seen or met her in person. She walks in, tiny, but with what an aura; she takes the podium, and there are those eyes that tell me another story.

She speaks but all I see is Else Lasker-Schüler — those eyes, the hands, the voice I hear is the voice I have imagined. The childlike sensibility enveloping and guarding the woman's sensuous presence: this is Else Lasker-Schüler. Malina speaks German, accent-free, and with the clarity of a bell. She is at the edge of a new life, having lost her partner, Julian Beck, only a few months before to cancer. I have something for her, and for her theatre — *IandI*, a play that needs her. I approach her after her lecture; she is marvelously approachable.

"Frau Malina. I have something for you that might be just right. You know Else Lasker-Schüler? Yes. Her poetry? Yes." She is curious. I tell her about the play, *IandI*. And a few months later, we are able to meet, to come together. I give her the text in German and I show her some visual materials — photographs of Lasker-Schüler, of Jerusalem, and photocopies from the Lasker-Schüler archives — some diary entries, some drawings and rhymes, and pages of the play's manuscript with Lasker-Schüler's markings on them. Finally, I show her a draft of my translation. We sit in her apartment, side by side, on a sofa. She tells me she is looking for a space for The Living Theatre in New York, after working many years abroad, in a kind of exile. "This play needs a home. Our theatre needs a home." It took four more years, until 1989, to find a home for both. And then there was Avenue C, the corner of Third Street.

"Come, take a seat, mein Freund, and watch this hellish play of my poetic art straight from the theatre of my heart." (*IandI*)

As The Living Theatre transformed a storefront into a magical home, members of the surrounding community came to watch this phantasmagoria of a play in rehearsals. The door was open; hearts were open. Rehearsals began during the summer after Judith and I worked on the text throughout the spring.

The challenge of *IandI* lies in its theatrical bravura. The poet, who opens the play and appears throughout as one of the characters, sets the scene in Gebe-Hinnom (derived from a Hebrew word for Hell), an actual natural theatre in Jerusalem, situated below the Tower of David. She welcomes Max Reinhardt, who has come from Hollywood to direct her play under the watchful eyes of King David and King Solomon. Within that context we find a theatrical hell where Faust and Mephisto ruminate about the presence or absence of God, as news reaches them about the world torn apart by the Nazis. The Nazi leaders eventually perish in a cataclysmic fireflood unleashed by Mephisto after he hosts the Nazis at a banquet. And all the while the Ritz Brothers perform their antics. It is truly a "theatrum mundi," structurally resembling a medieval mystery play with scenes as stations in the real and imaginary life of the poet, beginning with her flight from Germany in 1933, and ending with her death in 1945. The final station is a garden in Jerusalem where the Poet and the Scarecrow (another *IandI* duality) meet and the Poet comes to her final rest.

A Prologue in the Theatre and an Epilogue in Heaven complete the play, echoing Goethe's *Faust*. It took a special theatrical and poetic vision to give this play the arc it needed in production — from the exquisitely sublime to the horrendously ridiculous. I could not have asked for a more perfect melding than Judith Malina, The Living Theatre aesthetic, and that magic space on Avenue C. The theatre became a hellish cabaret — a repetitive loop of Ritz Brothers' movies was juxtaposed against live actors who transmogrified themselves from Ritz Brothers to Nazis (Goebbels, Goring, and Schirach etc.). A mad devil, the Reichstag arsonist, fiddled his way through the throng; a gorgeous Mephisto aroused Faust's longing with his melancholy cello; Marthe Schwerdtlein (alias Margaret) seduced Goebbels; and finally, a medieval wheel of misfortune unleashed a firebrand, which swallowed up the Nazi gang. Sitting at small tables in penumbral light, the audience was exposed to an ever-changing, all-encompassing event. The spirit of Else Lasker-Schüler's work was captured perfectly in this powerful mix of mischief, lyricism, and bold sensuality.

The paradox of *IandI* (*Ich und Ich*), is the I bonded to the I, that duality that implies individuality, an indivisible twosome that yearns to separate while striving to merge. It is the paradox of the actor, one who pretends to be another; it is the paradox of theatre, which is meant to be an immediate experience while it mediates another; it is the paradox of The Living Theatre, whose anarchic spirit strives to make one of a divided world. And it is the paradox of human life, moving inexorably forward while trying not to turn itself into a pillar of salt, as it contemplates the detritus left behind — all this became a living experience for me that summer of 1989.

A delicious coda was The Living Theatre tour of this production (in my English translation*) in Germany and Italy to great critical acclaim one year later. However, as I look back now in 1998, the soul of the event took shape at home in New York on Avenue C with a family of actors drawn from the existential playgrounds of New York's Heaven and Hell, watched over by the mother of them all, Judith/ Else.

---

* See Lasker-Schüler, Else. *IandI: A Theatrical Tragedy in Six Acts, a Prologue, and an Epilogue*. Translated by Beate Hein Bennett in: *The Divided Home/Land: Contemporary German Women's Plays*. Edited by Sue-Ellen Case. Ann Arbor: The University of Michigan Press, 1992.

# 4

## *THE BODY OF GOD*

Living on Third Street, feeling a part of the city, its pulse and its pains, we had from the outset been eager to attempt a particularly challenging collaboration: to create a play with the poorest of the poor, with the homeless sleeping sometimes in shelters, often on trains, in waiting-rooms or, when they were thrown out into the cold, on the subway grates where a little warmth could be found.

The project involved locating a dozen or so homeless people who were interested in spending most evenings at our storefront theater figuring out what it is they have to say about themselves and their situation and then putting it into theatrical form in partnership with a like number of Living Theatre actors.

Before we met with the homeless participants, the company discussed over several weeks how best to approach this contradiction-fraught collaboration. What kinds of training would work best for integrating the group? What sort of text would the piece evolve? What did we think we already knew about these people's situation? How could we ask them not to sleep in the theater? These were the questions we passed around our meeting circle, putting the chairs aside every so often to experiment on our feet.

Through advocacy organizations, we were put in touch with John Heuss House, a drop-in center in the financial district, where somewhere between 50 and a hundred displaced souls come for a daily hot meal, shower, medical attention and referral to one of the many houses of worship in the city offering cots for the night. Through the good offices of the reverend Win Peacock and Jennifer Barrows, who run the place with tough love, we were introduced to perhaps twenty of their clients, of whom eight joined our ensemble. They were:

CRYSTAL — a heavy-set woman with a brilliant smile and a story that revolved around medication

DWAYNE BAKER — a terribly shy, soft-voiced youth

LARRY WEISSMAN — the it-could-have-been-me emblem for the middle class — a smart Jewish guy from Flatbush who lost his wife, started drinking, lost his job, his apartment, and somewhere along the way, part of his mind

LEONA ETHERIDGE — an accomplished graphics designer waylaid by a series of foul blows, she did the poster and program for the show, and we hear she's back on her feet again

RAQUEL EXTRAVAGANZA — a wild transvestite streetwalker from the Bronx — shortly after opening in the show, she disappeared back into crack-smoking scenes

RENÉE JOHNSON — a big, lively woman with a temper — her story was of involuntary hospitalization in connection with carpal tunnel syndrome

SAMUEL BANKS — taciturn, warm-hearted, Sam was on medication to keep his mood swings within bounds — he often remained silent for hours

VIVI LA BELLA — a flamboyant transvestite who worked the street, Vivi couldn't help but get into trouble — she disappeared for a short while into jail after turning a fire extinguisher on an art show that she hated

To this group of Heuss House clients, one other self-identified homeless person who slept in church basements joined our ranks — a gifted, self-ordained preacher named Victor Donnell Roper. He wrote strange, passionate, evangelical sermons which he delivered regularly in parks and to our audience, as well.

During this preparatory time, several other people from the neighborhood who identified with the homeless joined the developing ensemble. Some were squatters, others had spent time in shelters; all were people living in marginal circumstances.

Bob Fass, a long-time late-night luminary at WBAI-FM, also joined the ensemble. Bob, a gifted actor of Shakespearean experience, had first performed with us as Leo Levy, the protagonist of Jerome Rothenberg's *Poland/1931*. He wanted to integrate a soliloquy from *King Lear* into the play, but graciously accepted my counsel against this idea, and instead recounted the true story of a local unfortunate who froze to death one night after the police made him put out the oil-drum fire that was keeping him alive.

From the beginning, then, we were really three groups: homeless people, Living Theatre actors, and local activists. On Sunday, February 11, 1990, we closed *IandI* and three days later, on Wednesday, we began six weeks of intensive rehearsal during which we became a single ensemble. Nightly, we gathered in a circle, exchanging life stories, and focusing our attention on the homeless participants' telling of how they landed on the street. These tales would form the basic sequence of the play's scenes. As director, I guided the group toward choosing a different theatrical form for each story. So, for example, Renée's sad tale became a blues ballad, Raquel and Vivi's, a striptease down to lacy lingerie, Leona's a series of strange games and Victor's, naturally, a sermon (with jazz sax accompaniment by William "Butch" Johnson).

We decided to perform the play in the space stripped bare. As the public entered, we "checked" their belongings into plastic bags which they were urged to keep with them, and presented them with pieces of cardboard to sit on, requiring them to move from place to place as the scenes unfolded in different locations. Carla Cubit, one of the few formerly homeless people in the neighborhood who had made her way into a squat, called the proceedings to order with a funky greeting all her own, "Good evenin' ladies n' gentlemen and welcome to The Livin' The-ay-ter.... My name is Carla and I have enjoyed workin' on this play very much and I learned a lot, too. We hope that you enjoy the play also and that you learn somethin' from it, too." The intensity and depth of the audience discussions within the play gave us reason to believe that many did.

## THE LIVING THEATRE

# THE BODY OF GOD

## COLLECTIVE CREATION WITH HOMELESS PEOPLE

Directed by Hanon Reznikov
Music by Joanie Fritz, Felipe Hernandez
Flyer Art by Leona Etheridge

"... The kinetic human sculptures that expand or contract like mechanized mantras-chanting sea-anemones... this is a Paradise Now for the 90's."
Village Voice

"An electric celebration .... It would take a heart of stone to be engulfed in one of these performances and not be moved."
Backstage

October 17 - November 11
Weds - Sun 7:30 PM
Admission $10/$7
students and seniors
Weds-Thurs:
Pay-what-you-can

## THE LIVING THEATRE 272 E. 3rd St. (East of Ave C)
Reservations and Information: (212) 979-0604

Fig. 11 *Body of God* Flyer

As one of the only people with a car, it fell to me to ferry the homeless actors from the drop-in center on Beaver Street to our Third Street rendezvous, and after the rehearsal or performance, to transport them on to the beds the Heuss Center had reserved for them in local churches. These were more comfortable arrangements than we would have been able to organize in our little room, and the homeless participants were content to have car service to their quarters. But at the start of every evening, it was necessary to coax our easily distracted homeless actors away from the drop-in center with its card games, television and especially, the complex social interaction which could easily drive the theater from their minds. And then there were the omnipresent temptations of booze and the crack pipe, both obtainable with little money on any street corner.

We had resolved early in our planning sessions that a nightly meal would be offered before the performance. A rotating kitchen schedule was laid out and a highly effective campaign with local restauranteurs led by local organizer Lynn Loflin yielded a plentiful supply of basic foodstuffs. The Heuss clients, however, arrived at the theater having already taken advantage of the drop-in center's late afternoon dinner, but after some cajoling, they were willing to sample the theater's vegetarian fare as well. For the struggling artists and squatters among us, the food counted more; for the homeless participants, it was more like a happy hour before the show.

And in the end, the play served best to strengthen the resolve of the homeless participants to make a life for themselves. Renée, Sam, and Leona, at least, have since let us know that they've found their way to jobs and apartments (Renée and Sam fell in love early on in rehearsals and have taken a place together). The squatters among us had a hard time persuading the homeless people to pursue the squatting alternative. The people sleeping in church basements felt that the situation of the squats was too precarious to be worth the sweat-equity effort. They were more eager to do time on waiting lists for city-owned apartments, especially as the rules mandated that the homeless be given priority for public housing, a situation not viewed kindly by the thousands of working poor families waiting for some rent relief. For the theater audience, it provided a warm moment of contact across forbidding socio-economic distances. For the neighborhood squatters and activists, it was a chance to come together around the problem of housing in a creative way. For the Living Theatre actors, creating and performing *The Body of God* was an informative, sobering phase in the continuing evolution of the company as an organism responsive to the issues surrounding us.

Though the project was conceived at the outset as culminating in a limited run of four weeks, we all felt that the results justified at least a second run the following season. Indeed, we felt that it deserved more than that — *The Body of God* deserved to continue in performance until better arrangements for the homeless were arrived at in New York City. But The Living Theatre on Third

Street had another destiny. The company was always determined to address a broad spectrum of concerns, social and philosophical, from the rarely-heard standpoint of pacifist anarchists. As compelling as the dilemma of the homeless is, it remained clear to us that we would not choose to become a single-issue group.

Nor did we consider it desirable to abandon the huge European audience which the company had developed since it began performing there in  And so just as we were sinking roots beneath the mean streets of the Lower East Side, we were organizing a return to Europe to present our newest work to the audience we had left seven years earlier, at the time that Julian Beck fell ill, after seven years spent exclusively in Europe. Because The Living Theatre's sense of itself has always been not as a local phenomenon, or community- specific enterprise, but rather as a libertarian presence afloat on the wind, a group which might just choose to give a performance in your backyard anytime, wherever you might happen to live. The first post-Julian Beck tour was accomplished from July through September, 1990 with *The Tablets* and *IandI* in Italy, Germany, Spain, and Czechoslovakia. They were The Living Theatre's first performances in a Europe much changed since our last appearance in 1983.

When the company returned to Berlin, we played on both sides of the defunct Wall. On that same tour we returned to Czechoslovakia for the first time since our clandestine Prague performance of 1980 (leaked soon after by *Nouvel Observateur*) to find that practically everybody who had attended the secret *Antigone* were now running the government, except for Havel, who missed it because he was in jail at the time. The following spring we brought *Rules of Civility* to Hungary and Italy, where the play had its greatest impact during the days of the First Gulf War. In Rome, we led the candle-bearing audience to the gates of the American Embassy, where we were met by police battalions bent on stilling our protest but rendering it instead all the more photogenic to a sympathetic press.

Fig. 12
*Body of God*: Exavier Wardlaw Muhammad   *[Photo: Ira Cohen]*

# THE BODY OF GOD

Collective creation of The Living Theatre Company
in collaboration with
homeless people of the Lower East Side of Manhattan


directed and written down by
Hanon Reznikov

March 1990


### I — The Noplace Place

[Tableau of the Homeless and their Life's Baggage — Homeless Ensemble
(HE) and the bags they carry with them each day
as they travel from shelter to shelter]


CARLA/DWAYNE
[welcoming Audience (A) at the door and introducing her/himself
to this performance of *The Body of God* at The Living Theatre. I'm
Carla/Dwayne and I have been/am a homeless person... [continues ad lib]

[Living Theatre Ensemble (LTE) approaches A, distributes cardboard seats,
checks A's possessions into shopping bags]


SPEAKER 1
The ritual, a unity of primeval origins, makes possible
an almost unlimited rising higher.


SPEAKER 2
The ritual can overtake nature and penetrate into the biostructure of the body.


SPEAKER 3
The ritual is an experience of unification.

*113*

CARLA/DWAYNE
[as the last A members find seats]
... and I hope we'll all learn something together tonight.
Now, if we're all here, we can begin.

## II — The Obstacle Cantata

[percussion rhythm — Entire Ensemble (E) moves through space
as community-in-the-making searching and confronting obstacles —
individual enactments become collective efforts]

SPEAKERS
If only we could remember that we share a common source, one mother...
If only I were the mayor...

[unison action, then searching the ensemble]

If only I could get a decent job...
If only the air weren't poisoned...

[unison action, then searching the sky]

If only I had turned left instead of right...

If only I had my green card...

[unison action, then searching the audience]

If only I could stay warm...
If only I could see beyond the smiles...

[unison action, then searching the ensemble]

If only I was a woman...
If only the words 'if only' were not a part of my vocabulary...

[unison action, then searching the sky]

If only I had the cash to perform all the time...
If only I weren't afraid to look at you directly in the eye...

[unison action, then searching the audience]

If only I didn't have to run from the government...

Ritual III — **The Rise and Exorcism of the Many-Headed Demon
Without a Home**

LTE separates A from HE with barrier tape as HE transforms into Many-
Headed Demon Without a Home — LTE separation chant/menacing A possessions — Carol/Cenen tells her story — HE chant: we are your nightmare

Ritual IV — **The Rise & Exorcism of The Many-Headed Demon
Without a Home**

E forms Circle of Love around Raquel and Vivi — R and V tell their stories,
dressing to Go Out — E confronts R & V with Death Dance
of Sexual Disgust — R & V cruise the house

GARY
This is a scene we created with Vivi and Raquel. Vivi and Raquel were with
us until a few days ago. Now Vivi is in jail and Raquel has disappeared.

LOUIS
We hope they will be back soon, but until then, we want to keep their spirit
with us here. These are the words they wrote.

When Vivi dresses, she becomes the hottest bitch on campus.

When Raquel dresses, she puts on a fuck-me dress and drop-dead lipstick.

When Vivi dresses, she makes herself the…

When Raquel dresses, she turns into the most beautiful pussy in Manhattan.

When Vivi goes out, she's looking to swallow ten inches or more.

When Raquel goes out, she's looking for a big black man who'll slam-fuck her
all night long.

When Vivi goes out, she's looking to eat out a hot man's asshole.

When Raquel goes out, she's looking for a man who will fuck her brains out.

When Vivi goes out, she finds... herself.

When Raquel goes out, she finds... herself.

### Ritual V — **The Occult Rites of Money**

E performs Mystical Numerical Rites as Leona tells her story —
the measurement of need, the measurement of food, the measurement
of resistance to authority

### Ritual VI — **Death by Cold**

E imposes silence on A — E forces James and Sam to keep moving
as they tell of the quiet ones who never make it inside... and of the cold
— E recruits A to walk for the ones that die out there

### Ritual VII — **Blue Woman**

Renee sings her Blues — E counterpoint of Greed and Contempt — Living
Theatre Ensemble retreats in horror from Sam's body until they reach the
walls, when they clutch the walls in fear

HOMELESS ENSEMBLE REMAINS CLOSE BY SAM,
GRIEVING/RENEE SINGS:

It's a complete emptiness of the heart
Lost within a heartless world
Each day that passes by
Is like the drifting sea going to and fro

People giving nickels and dimes
Nobody giving a home to the poor
Just watching nothing but time

Death is the only key to the door

RENEE SPEAKS

LIVING THEATRE ENSEMBLE:
Woman, you are crazy
You are crazy, woman
Break
Break
Join us
Buy it

Buy us
Join us
Join us
Kick the swine
Up to our litters
on the back of the swine

HOMELESS ENSEMBLE HEALS SAM/RENEE SINGS:
Insane and insanity combine as one
Drugs and alcoholic struggle the battle
Yet these victims have no life
Cause the world has crushed them to no end,
then replies, well done

RENEE SPEAKS

LIVING THEATRE ENSEMBLE:
Crazy woman
Crazy woman
buy in

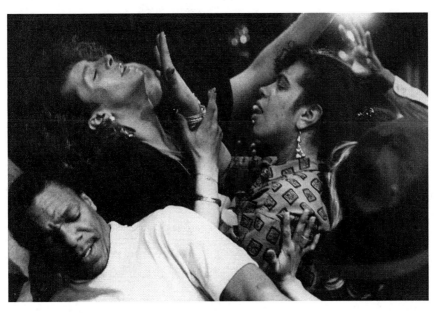

Fig. 13
*Body of God:* (left to right) Johnson Anthony,
Raquel Extravaganza, Vivi Labella  *[Photo: Ira Cohen]*

before it's too late
and we leave you
to the bag people
and the street fires
then take you simpering and reeking to Bellevue
where nobody will find you
you, crazy woman
you

HOMELESS ENSEMBLE RAISES SAM/RENEE SINGS:
Homeless without a care in this harsh world
And no true judgment from humanity
Causes the heart to be hard
Causes the mind to work overtime

What little reality is left within someone
Shows that yet there is hope
The battle is to strive and survive
To create and make the dream your goal

Ritual VIII — **The Absolute Collective**

E invites A into unifying rite of Touch and Voice — Body of God/Body of
Being — Victor's Vision — Necessity returns focus from future to present as
bags must be retrieved, night's shelter secured

My name is Larry. I have been homeless since June of 1990, but that story
begins way before then. I had it very good once. I came from a nice family.
I got a Masters degree in psychology, an executive job in a bank, a beautiful
wife and two beautiful children. Then in 1980 I got divorced. From that point
on all that I had and felt did not mean anything. I became more and more
depressed. I lost my job, my apartment and I almost lost my family. For the
next eight years I bounced from job to job and apartment to apartment.

Finally in September 1989 I walked out of my apartment for the last time.
I walked the streets for two days until as a last resort I signed myself
into a hospital for help. I spent the next three months there. I was released
in December 1989, but the fact is that I was still not capable
of fending for myself.

For the next five months I lived at a friend's house, but he also had emotional
problems. Both of us were not working — the rent was not being paid and we

had very little food. I was not living, just existing.
Finally, on June 12, 1990 we were evicted.

For the first time in my life I was really homeless. I kept asking, "why is this happening to me?" I was very frightened of the streets. I did not think I could survive. I walked into a police station and asked for help. They told me that I may just have to sleep in the park. At that moment I felt like all hope was lost.

But I was more fortunate than a lot of homeless people. I found a city agency that brought me to the shelter that I am in today. There I have a roof over my head and plenty of food to eat. My future is still up in the air, but now I can start working on creating my own life. You see, before I became homeless, I was only doing what I was told to do. Now I want to make my own decisions.

My name is Parvaneh, and this is what I wrote about the first days of four months I spent in city shelters this year.

[chorus]

1. I went to the shelter under the influence of a superhuman inspiration. I had just come to New York and was a guest at a friend's house. The host was getting impatient with me and one night when I came home after two weeks of tension, she gave me one week's notice. I was indignant at the short notice and anxious to show I did not need the one-week grace period.

My inspiration was Malcolm X, who was the only connection I had to New York. I was born in a Muslim family in Teheran and had read Malcolm's autobiography four years ago and so I knew that there is an Islamic community in New York. I hoped I could enter one of their communities in New York, but when I asked the young Muslim brother who sets his table of incense, books, and beads at the 14th Street station, he told me, "Our communities are for ourselves." Being a Muslim and being from Iran did not make a difference.

He pointed at another brother, "That brother there lives in a shelter." The word "shelter" was the magic word. It led me in a new direction.

[chorus]

2. I took the number 6 train to Broadway–Lafayette and walked into 350 Lafayette, a halfway house for women who have been in state mental institutions. This is a referral place for all those who first enter the shelter system. All women are referred to Brooklyn Women's Shelter in East New York,

where the women are assigned a case worker, interviewed and assessed according to their needs and abilities.

I am waiting for the van to Brooklyn. The woman I talked to, Barbara Walker, told me my name has been phoned in and that they have assigned me a New York City homeless number, I will be able to leave during the day to look for a job — they will give me tokens for that. She tells me the shelter is not a nice place — there is theft, some of the women are criminals or mentally disturbed. I am having second thoughts, but tonight I am afraid of nothing.

Another woman waits with me. She reads the newspaper and looks tired. I ask her if she likes almonds. She does. I offer her some. She doesn't want any. There are six security video monitors in a booth on our left. There is a strong smell of disinfectant. I feel I am in a performance acting as the artist who acts homeless. This cushion of thought saves me from losing my nerve.

[chorus]

3. 11 p.m. Brooklyn Women's Shelter is a wasteland, over-crowded and understaffed, in a state of constant frenzy... All of a sudden I feel sick. What am I doing in this horrible place. I feel like running to the phone and telling someone I am here and that I have made a mistake. But I am here out of a real situation. I do not have a place to stay. In this society where everything is designed to have an end, I do not know what the outcome of this situation is going to be.

I am assigned a dorm with twenty-four other women. I was assigned bed #4 but someone was sleeping in it. Bed #5 was empty and I was told it was ok to sleep there, but when the next shift came for the bed check, they tried to get me out of bed #5, and the sleeping woman out of bed #4, and had us exchange sheets and beds. I objected and we went to the office. I hope there will be someone there who will have more sense. We knocked and a tall woman in a yellow raincoat and pink lipstick opened the door. "Isn't it easier to change numbers on a piece of paper than to change sheets and people from bed to bed?"

She agreed and I came back triumphantly to bed #5 which is next to a window and offers a little light after they turn out the lights. I took off my skirt. I was in a black shirt and black underpants. A woman stopped me, "You're cute. How long you been here?" I asked her if she slept with women. She said she didn't but she wanted to sleep with me. I said I was in bed #5. And I said good night.

[chorus]

4. A woman bursts into the dorm. "I'm outta here," she screams and takes her suitcase. A group of guards comes in after her. "You wanna fuck with me? I'm outta here!"

Some in the dorm say she shouldn't have left. Where is she going to go? The woman two beds over wants to club her husband to death for having taken twelve years of her life and her children. She is very bitter.

I walk in the corridors wanting something. Subdued by the male guards and desiring the women who desire me. I want to get lost in their world. To go drinking with them and to do the wild things they do — to fuck under the shower at night, invite them to my bed after lights-out.

[chorus]

5. This morning I have a flash of understanding that my bed is one among many in this place. I will accept no one else's judgment, and no one can force me off my path. I hope I will soon be born into the human race, into its core where its pains and ecstasies are. Life that does not encompass other people's existence is an illusion. The current of other lives flows under the base of each life and when currents flow violently or disorderly, the columns of illusions break.

Tomorrow I will go to 168th Street and Broadway to visit the Audubon ballroom, where Malcolm X was shot. Maybe I will get a glimpse of what Malcolm's inspiration is all about.
It's a complete emptiness of the heart
Lost within a heartless world
Each day that passes by
Is like the drifting sea going to and fro

People giving nickels and dimes
Nobody giving a home to the poor
Just watching nothing but time
Death is the only key to the door

Insane and insanity combine as one
Drugs and alcoholic struggle the battle
Yet these victims have no life
Cause the world has crushed them to no end,
then replies, well done

Homeless without a care in this harsh world
And no true judgment from humanity
Causes the heart to be hard
Causes the mind to work overtime

What little reality is left within someone
Shows that yet there is hope
The battle is to strive and survive
To create and make the dream your goal

— Renee Johnson

## THE ABSOLUTE COLLECTIVE (sc. 8)

SAM: It isn't too late for us — we're still here.

"BODY OF GOD — BODY OF BEING" CHANT BEGINS

SAM EXTENDS HAND TOWARD LIVING THEATRE ENSEMBLE
MEMBER AT WALL VICTOR JOINS LIVING THEATRE ENSEMBLE
MEMBER'S HAND TO SAM'S

VICTOR:

Hold on to the picture
Hold on to the picture
Until it comes into view

Do not even take a price
Do not even take a price
Until you know who is who

My name is Victor and I have chosen to be homeless
Because I will not allow my energy and time to be used for things I do not believe in.

ENSEMBLE BEGINS SLOW FORMATION OF CELLS
MOVEMENT/ENSEMBLE:
Capitalism is organized irreality, an established emptiness
Autonomy means irreducibility, it completely shuts out the strata

below
Body means complete openness

VICTOR:
Follow the morning star
Follow the morning star
And I will give it to you

We call for equal rights
We call for equal rights

For all mankind

LIVING THEATRE ENSEMBLE AND HOMELESS ENSEMBLE
UNITE IN CELLS/ENSEMBLE:
The spirit of capitalism is the most radical atheism ever formulated
What is owned will decay
The organic, with suddenness like an explosion, forms itself

VICTOR, THEN ENSEMBLE AUDIENCE
INTO CELLS FORMATION:
Hold on to the picture
Hold on to the picture
Until it comes into view

ENSEMBLE COMPLETES UNIFICATION
WITH AUDIENCE/ENSEMBLE:
Body is never private, it is never without people
a new body is needed
without adding a dimension, there is no exit

VICTOR:
All of God's children feel so much better
so much better
so much better
so much better now

CHANT DEVELOPS INTO CHORD

AT END OF CHORD, HOMELESS ENSEMBLE BREAK FORMA-
TION, GATHER THEIR BAGS IN THE MIDDLE OF THE SPACE

VICTOR: We're still here.

RENEE: We're working hard on helping ourselves.
LEONA: And we're praying to God that we'll get there together.
RAQUEL: But right now we have to go.
VIVI: There's a curfew at the shelters where we sleep.
CAROL: So we're leaving.
DWAYNE: Please don't forget us.
SAM: Take care of yourselves.

HOMELESS ENSEMBLE PICKS UP BAGS,
SAYS "GOOD NIGHT" AND WALKS OUT

BLACKOUT.

# 5
# GERMAN REQUIEM

*G*erman Requiem, an adaptation by Eric Bentley of Heinrich von Kleist's *Familien Schroffenstein,* was a peculiar artifact of the Third Street years. Bentley had gone at the mass of weighty plot and prose of the Kleist original with delicacy and verve, liberating from the raw material a finely wrought play about the tragic consequences of blind service to the vengeance cycle. With fratricidal wars multiplying around the globe, Malina saw in the play the potential to bring home to the audience's heart a choose-love-eschew-violence message as cogently as does *Romeo and Juliet.* She envisioned a staging that would divide the audience as well as performers into the rival camps of the feuding families, Varvand and Rosset.

Ilion Troya crafted a magnificent set for the occasion, splitting the rectangular space along its long axis and building two castle- like environments along twin narrow platforms running the length of the room. Between them, at the deep end of the space, stood a mountain wilderness where the lovers would meet first by chance, then in secret. The mountain was a wonderful little bit of Renaissance stage machinery, a naturalistic painted surface of stiffened fabric over a metal frame, complete with an electrically driven waterfall.

Later in the play, the whole mountain would lift open to reveal a cavern beneath. All the constructions and wall surfaces were given a painterly treatment by Ilion that underscored the storybook charm of the setting. It was surely our most elaborate and ingeniously constructed set at Third Street.

But somewhere along the way, the staging failed to involve the audience actively enough to overcome the fairy-tale remove of the play. Part of the problem was our not creating separate audience situations for the two camps — only at the front end of the space, for which Bentley had supplied twenty tall upholstered swivel chairs, was the public seated in distinct opposition, the action swirling off the lateral platforms and into the open space between them.

There was one memorable evening when the play came alive to a frightening degree. During the intermission, the audience gathered in the lobby saw through the storefront windows two gangs of warriors armed with clubs fly at each other from opposite ends of the street and flail at each other furiously for a few terrifying moments before fleeing the scene, leaving several wounded stricken on the asphalt. Only when the ambulances arrived and began carting away the injured did it become clear to everyone that what had happened was not part of the play, not staged for "Living Theatre" effect.

But it was also an experience that proved the play's validity for us — nothing could have bared the ferocious truth of the horrors of the vendetta more compellingly.

In the end the production looked more traditional in style than almost anything The Living Theatre has ever done. This was in no way helped by the costuming, the weakest element of the production. Bénédicte Leclerc, whose costumes graced *The Tablets* and *IandI*, had returned to France to have a baby. We were foolish enough to dress everybody in shabby approximations of period costume garnered from donations. The actors, however, held their ground firmly. Pat Russell and Gary Brackett made a tremendously engaging pair, boldly revealing their naked bodies at the play's climax as the lovers switch costumes to escape detection. Tom Walker and Robert Projansky were powerfully seignorial as the heads of the feuding houses, and Amber and Laura Kolb evoked compassion for their troubled ladies, and then there was a whole constellation of wonderful characterizations, including Joanie Fritz Zosike's terrorized maidservant, Michael Saint Clair's swashbuckling cavalier, Alan Arenius' hapless

Figure 14: *German Requiem:* Amber and Tom Walker *[Photo: Ira Cohen]*

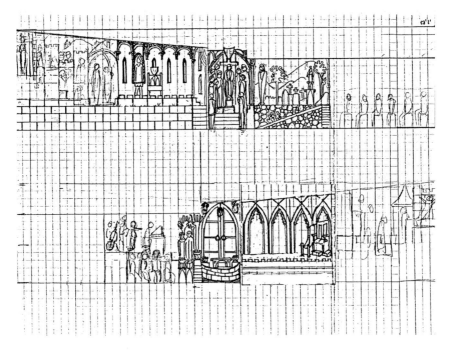

Figure 15: *German Requiem:* Early sketch of Ilion Troya's design,
showing lateral walls of the set.

towerkeep, Bobby Hieger's lovestruck boy, Maria Hurtado's soulful peasant
girl, Bob Paton's other-worldly elder statesman (Bentley had actually persuaded
me to call Quentin Crisp and ask him to play this last, but Quentin demurred
sweetly, "But, I'd have to be at all the performances, wouldn't I? And then there
would be all those rehearsals.... Oh dear, no, I don't think so.").

As we began the European tour with *The Tablets* and *IandI* a couple of
months after opening *German Requiem*, we decided to rehearse a second cast and
run the play through the summer while the original company was away. We
were quite proud to be driving around Europe in minibuses again while performances continued at our New York home. This created some problems.
While a few gems emerged from the second cast of *German Requiem* — Stuart
Williams' dashingly sensitive young leading man, Charles Craigin's Artaudian
seer and Lou Bellucci's high-strung emissary among them — the general level of
performance suffered from the absence of the original cast, and perhaps, from
that of the director. And there were troubled feelings within the group about
the company's having created a less-than-equal extension of itself.

# THE RULES OF CIVILITY
## Scene Six - The Insurrection
### Excerpts - Vocal Duets - Parts

text: George Washington
**music: Patrick Grant**

Figure 16: *Rules of Civility*
Song sheet from the score by Patrick Grant

# 6

# RULES OF CIVILITY

During the winter of 1990–91, we took it upon ourselves to stage a curious document by George Washington called *Rules of Civility and Decent Behavior in Company and in Conversation.* Judith and I happened upon this list of 110 rules for proper conduct at the souvenir counter at Valley Forge National Monument, where curiosity bade us stop en route to Bryn Mawr College, Judith having been awarded a fellowship for a two-week residency there. It was an idea that came of a sudden. "I think I can make a play out of this," I mused, fingering the faux-parchment pages in fascination. "Yes," Judith smiled, "I believe you can."

The text, a version of a 16th-century Jesuitical text thought to have been given as a copying exercise to the 13-year old Washington by his tutor, was taken to heart by young George, who in later years is said to have made copies of it for his family, and perhaps even to have passed it off as his own composition. It reveals what appears to us as a media-age sensibility whose primary concern is never morality, but is, instead, public image. The purely ethical value of an action is never called into question, only its effect on the onlookers' perception. The rules are designed exclusively to ensure respectability, but perhaps what enthused young George most was the way in which they attempt to balance finer feelings with grosser realities. Thus expressions of deeply-felt idealism like "Labor to keep alive in your breast that little spark of celestial fire called conscience" are found alongside class-conscious admonitions like "In speaking to men of quality do not lean nor look them full in the face, nor approach too near them."

To amplify the consequences of this tension, Washington appears throughout the play simultaneously as two people: the pubescent student and the elder statesman. The boy delights in devising an order for an ideal world; the man uses the rules to organize his dominance.

To provide a structure susceptible of dramatic development, a schism develops among the 14-member ensemble as they present the rules to the audience. They divide into two antagonistic factions: white men on the one hand (the Empowered), and on the other, women and people of color (the Excluded). The Washingtons use the rules to secure the advantage of their own kind. In a kind of scenic premonition of the action to follow, the ensemble is seen in the play's first moment as composed of two opposing factions on a blind collision course. The ensemble then unites around the doubled figure of Washington, and broadcasts his vision of the world order to the audience. As the play develops, the ensemble descends into the audience area and makes direct, proselytizing contact with members of the public.

From the first scene, the actors voice their awareness of the play's Pirandellian situation — even when they speak Washington's words, they are ever-aware of being The Living Theatre using the ironic device of the rules to propagandize its own vision of reality, but this makes them no less of a brigade of American cultural impresarios foisting their agenda on the public. At length, however, subversive, "excluded" elements of the ensemble enjoin the audience to reject the imposition of the rules by the "empowered." This rebellion builds musically to a climactic concert at which the Empowered perform a cacophonous instrumental work woven between songs raising the pedestrian language of the rules to lyrical heights. Joanie Fritz Zosike, Robert Hieger, and Michael Saint Clair were memorably adept at making musical magic of formulations like "Don't sit at the head of the table unless it is your proper place." As the concert proceeds, the two Washingtons are seated onstage at a little table where they dissect and consume a pineapple, symbol of colonial wealth. The ensemble, meanwhile, is out in the house, in agonized struggle with huge lengths of military camouflage cloth which engulfs them. The confrontation concludes with a desperate exhortation, "Break the rules!" followed by a final sequence of minimalistic, often comic vignettes, played out in small, intimate encounters meant to remind us how the rules of behavior reach into our everyday lives. There follows an epilogue in the form of a candlelit vigil in the street outside the theater — an anti-war demonstration conducted as a silent meditation on the consequences of Washington's thinking in the real world.

The principal means of expression in the play are choreographic and musical. The text of the rules themselves, which constitutes something like 95% of the words, when not joined with the music in song, functions as a series of opera-style supertitles.

The production became an occasion to redeem from cold storage in a Tribeca cellar rented from Tibetan Buddhists the muslin backdrop and wings which Julian had hand-painted for our 1980 Munich production of Ernst Toller's *Masse-Mensch*. Tall muted panels of dusky green ribbed with vertical strokes of grey and black, this was a Beck design originally intended to suggest the bleak, prison-like world of factory workers. But when the drapes came to surround our sprightly song-and-dance ritual presentation of the Rules, the space became eerily evocative of the clearing in the Virginia woods where the young Washington laid the text to paper.

Patrick Grant composed a brilliantly energetic score for the play. Driven by live piano (played at full tilt by Patrick himself like a carnivalesque master-of-musical-ceremonies) and synthesized rhythmic riffs, the music for *Rules of Civility* was more deeply embedded in the staging and in the company's consciousness than any written score with which I can remember our working.

During the winter of 1990–91, as we were constructing our staging of *Rules*, the United States responded to the Iraqi invasion of Kuwait with a full-scale air-sea-and-land assault. Before the land war began, the wisdom of sending in American troops in order to guarantee the Emir of Kuwait protection of his assets was widely questioned across the country. Washington's renowned Farewell Address at Fraunces Tavern rang in my ears. "Beware of foreign entanglements," he had cautioned. We participated in the sizeable demonstrations taking place at the U.N., under whose aegis the military adventure in the Persian Gulf was to be organized. During these months, Judith was in Los Angeles, stuck on the Paramount lot filming *The Addams Family*. I would call her from the heart of the New York demonstrations, holding the cell phone aloft so that she could hear the crowd chanting "No Blood for Oil." She did manage to participate in the LA demonstrations in front of the Federal Building on Wilshire Boulevard. From either shore of the continent, we watched with bated breath as Congress approved the war by a minuscule margin. And yet from the day the bombing began, all mainstream opposition to the war evaporated. As happens during wars, opposition to the attack was seen as disloyal to the troops whose lives were on the line. Our candlelight vigil outside the theater at play's end became a protest against Operation Desert Storm (at first called Desert Shield, until the ground war began), to which we invited the audience as we interrupted the curtain calls to light our candles before striding down the aisles and out into the street. We spread ourselves over the four corners of the intersection of Third Street and Avenue C, holding candles stuck through paper cup-windshields and standing motionless through ten minutes of silence, meditating on the elusiveness of peace and of the rules that might lead there.

The production marked another attempt to keep the company working simultaneously in New York and in Europe. But unlike the period when *German Requiem* ran on with a replacement cast while the senior members of the group went off to recreate *The Tablets* and *IandI* in Europe, *Rules* was double-cast from the outset and rehearsed on a double-schedule: afternoons, we worked on the home version, and in the evenings, we rehearsed it all in Italian except for the songs, which we decided to leave in English. And this time, the first-string cast never played at Third Street. We left for Rome a few days before the New York première, Judith remaining moored on *The Addams Family* set the whole time, working hard for the money that was keeping The Living Theatre afloat. Unfortunately, the New York cast never did achieve the precision and clarity that excited the Europeans. I did have a special affection nonetheless for the masquelike quality of the New York performances on the miniature proscenium stage we built at the rear end of the space. Michael Shenker, a talented musician and committed community activist, ran the show in New York, using a synthesizer set in clavichord mode which created a special, period kind of elegance unlike Patrick Grant's music-hall acoustic piano, although Patrick's razor-sharp, driving sense of rhythm infused the actors

**RULES OF CIVILITY
AND DECENT BEHAVIOR IN
COMPANY AND CONVERSATION**

*by George Washington*

**put not your Hands
to any Part of the
Body not usually
Discovered**

**THE
LIVING
THEATRE**

Figure 17: *Rules of Civility* Program cover

onstage with an obsessional dynamism that set the play aglow on tour and somehow, was bombastic in a way well suited to the "we'll tell you how to behave" attitude inherent in the text and gave it epic stature.

As with so much of The Living Theatre's work, *Rules* had greater impact abroad than at home. We recreated the show two years later, after the Third Street theater was shut down, first for a series of performances at Theater for the New City and then for a six-city tour in Germany and Hungary. On Third Street, Michael Strong was an appealingly self-absorbed elder Washington and Lauren Wissot an agreeably spontaneous Boy George, but it was in the touring production, thanks to the finely-wrought performances of Tom Walker and Isha Manna Beck, that the Washingtons became a frighteningly authentic pair.

In Italy, *Rules* enjoyed the great fortune of being the right play in the right place at the right time. From the moment we arrived in Rome in mid-January, public doubts among Italians and other Europeans about the American rhetoric justifying the Gulf War were widespread. Teatro delle Arti, where we opened *Rules* in Rome, is a large, elegant theater just off the Via Veneto and just a few blocks away from the American Embassy. It seemed natural that our candle-light vigil at show's end should become a procession to that destination, where we were confronted by an armada of police and military vehicles, to the particular delight of the press. "Is it possible that they are still there, outside the American Embassy, protesting the American War, just as they did in the 60's? Yes, it is possible — and it is necessary!" (*L'Espresso*). When the candlelight procession of actors and audience arrived at the Embassy gates and the joined forces of Carbinieri and Polizia Municipale demanded that we disperse, we dissolved into the night to the cheers of the marchers. It was also the first time that The Living Theatre had toured a play in which neither Beck nor Malina had had a hand, and it was heartening to see the company hit the mark all the same.

# RULES OF CIVILITY AND DECENT BEHAVIOR IN COMPANY AND IN CONVERSATION

by George Washington

adapted by Hanon Reznikov

The Living Theatre
1991


Scene 1 — THE MISSION


[Ensemble ("E") strides onto stage, looking straight ahead, then turning sharply toward the audience. Music establishes a seductively regular rhythm — an almost mechanical pulse. E makes successive waves of Signs of Respect toward audience ("A")]

DIRECTOR
Rule no. 1: Every action done in company ought to be with some sign of respect to those present.

[Sign of Respect for the Presence of Others]

VOICE FROM ENSEMBLE
The Rules of Civility and Decent Behavior in Company and Conversation are tools for the conquest of power through the management of perception.

[Sign of Respect for the Self]

VOICE FROM ENSEMBLE
Rule no. 2: Don't put your hands to any part of the body not usually uncovered.

[Sign of Respect for Authority]

### VOICE FROM ENSEMBLE
This play is the product of The Living Theatre, an American corporation
registered in the state of New York.

[Sign of Respect for God]

### VOICE FROM ENSEMBLE
20: The gestures of the body must be suited to your discourse.

[Sign of Respect for Territory]

### VOICE FROM ENSEMBLE
New York City was the first capital of the United States. Here, George
Washington was inaugurated the country's first president in 1789
at Federal Hall, only steps away from the current home
of the New York Stock Exchange.

[Sign of Respect for the audience's Ability to Pay]

### VOICE FROM ENSEMBLE
The Living Theatre has a strategy. An anarchist strategy
to uncover the Mystery of the Rules.

[E begins Conformity Square Dance]

### VOICE FROM ENSEMBLE
Washington built his career with steadiness and precision from the time he
was a boy. When he was 13, he wrote out a numbered list of the 110 rules for
proper behavior.

[BOY WASHINGTON appears in the house, steps onto the stage,
E pauses in dance, BOY WASHINGTON addresses A]

### BOY WASHINGTON
Rule no. 5: If you have to cough, sneeze, sigh or yawn, don't do it out loud.
Do it privately.
[E resumes dance]

### VOICE FROM ENSEMBLE
The Rules appear to be derived from an English translation of a set of Rules
written by Jesuits in France more than a century before. It is supposed that

young Washington's teacher must have assigned him the Rules as a copying task. Some scholars credit this unknown teacher with the selection and ordering of this version. Others prefer to credit George Washington himself.

BOY WASHINGTON
80: Don't be so tedious in your discourse.

VOICE FROM ENSEMBLE
The Living Theatre's strategy for revolution depends
on proving that the social structure is too rigid.

[WASHINGTON THE MAN appears from the wings and addresses E]

WASHINGTON THE MAN
61: Stuff not your discourse with sentences. [pause, then to A]
24: Don't laugh too loud or too much at any public spectacle.

VOICE FROM ENSEMBLE
This rigidity is best expressed in numbers.

WASHINGTON THE MAN
73: Think before you speak.

ENSEMBLE
Rule no. 6:
Don't sleep when others speak.
Don't sit when others stand.
Don't speak when you should hold your peace.
Don't walk on when others stop... (repeats...)

BOY WASHINGTON
4: Don't hum to yourself and don't tap your fingers or feet.

VOICE FROM ENSEMBLE
Washington adopted the Rules of Civility as a strategy for a successful career.
They made him "the father of his country." He published copies and gave
them to his family. They pointed the way to a kind of mission.

WASHINGTON THE MAN
If the conduct of Americans, while promoting their own happiness
should influence the feelings of other nations
[E stops, turns toward A]

WASHINGTON THE MAN
And thereby render a service to mankind,
the Americans will receive a double pleasure.

[E smiles out toward A]

ENSEMBLE
82: Be careful to keep your promise.

**Scene 2 — ASSEMBLY**

[latecomers are seated]

VOICE FROM ENSEMBLE
8: It's good manners to make space for latecomers.

VOICE FROM ENSEMBLE
W. The Living Theatre are preparing. Preparing to encounter you, our audience, again. The Rules concern how we are seen. What you make of us is
what we are.

[E forms into Grooming Groups that tenderly arrange each other. The women
put neckties on the men. The men tie sashes around the women's waists.
They sing.]

Rule the thirteenth:
Don't kill vermin,
Ticks or fleas,
In the sight of others.

And if you see any filth
Or thick spittle
Put your foot on it
Dexterously.

Keep your nails clean and short,
Keep your hands and teeth clean
But when you do, don't seem to show
Any great concern,
Says rule 15.

Don't wear clothes

That are foul and ripped
See that they're brushed once a day
That's rule fifty-one.

Don't puff up your cheeks
Says rule sixteen
Don't loll your tongue about —

Don't puff up your cheeks
Says rule sixteen
Don't loll your tongue about —

Don't rub your hands
Or stroke your beard
Bite your lips
Or leave them unclosed.

Oh, don't kill vermin
Ticks or fleas
In the sight of others.

[WASHINGTON THE BOY is adjusting
the appearance of WASHINGTON THE MAN]

WASHINGTON THE MAN
Keep to the fashion of your equals.

WASHINGTON THE BOY
Fifty-two!

VOICE FROM ENSEMBLE
The acute attention to social rank and to one's own place within that ranking
constitute an essential awareness of the culture.
[E begins the Giving and Taking of Place]

VOICE FROM ENSEMBLE
32: You are to offer the chief place to your equal.

VOICE FROM ENSEMBLE
And he to whom it is offered ought to at first refuse it.

VOICE FROM ENSEMBLE
But at the second asking he should accept it.

VOICE FROM ENSEMBLE
But at the second asking he should accept it.

VOICE FROM ENSEMBLE
But not without acknowledging his own unworthiness.

ENSEMBLE
32.

VOICE FROM ENSEMBLE
31: If anyone far surpasses others in estate and yet would give his place to an
inferior, the other ought not to accept it.

VOICE FROM ENSEMBLE
And it should be offered with much earnestness.

VOICE FROM ENSEMBLE
Nor offered more than once or twice.

ENSEMBLE
31.

VOICE FROM ENSEMBLE
The great have precedence in all places, especially those in office.
They are in dignity. 33.

[Giving and Taking of Place ends in the formation of the Great Pyramid.
Those at top close ranks in silent conference. E strains to hear.]

WASHINGTON THE BOY
84: When your superiors are talking, don't listen in, or speak or laugh.

EXCLUDED
35: Let your discourse be short and comprehensive.

VOICES FROM THE TOP OF THE PYRAMID
In company of those of higher quality than yourself,
speak not until you are asked. 85.
[E performs Rite of Entreaty]

WASHINGTON THE BOY
Persons of low degree — 36 — ought not to use many ceremonies
to others of high degree.

WASHINGTON THE MAN

But those of high degree — 36 again — ought to treat those of low degree
without arrogance. Rule nineteen says keep a pleasant expression on your
face, though in serious matters, somewhat grave.

[Everyone puts on a perique, faces each other and chants,
talking wigs off and putting them on as they feel themselves required.]

26: In Pulling of your Hat to Persons of Distinction, as Noblemen, Justices,
Churchmen &c make a Reverence, bowing more or less according to the
Custom of the Better Bred, and Quality of the Person. Amongst your equals
expect not always that they Should begin with you first, but to Pull off the
Hat when there is no need of Affectation, in the Manner of Saluting and
resaluting in words to keep to the most usual Custom.

27: Tis ill manners to bid one more eminent than yourself to be covered as
well as not to do it that makes too much haste to Put on his hat does not well,
yet he ought to Put it on at the first, or at most the Second time of being ask'd;
now what is herein Spoken, of Qualification in behaviour in Saluting, ought
also to be observed in taking of Place, and Sitting down for ceremonies
without Bounds is troublesome.

ENSEMBLE

And Sitting down for the ceremonies without Bounds is troublesome.

WASHINGTON THE BOY

If anyone comes to speak to you while you are sitting, stand up, even if he is
your inferior.

ENSEMBLE (rising)
28!

## Scene 3 — THE VISITATION

[WASHINGTON THE BOY produces a pineapple.
One of the ENSEMBLE screams at the sight — s/he is possessed of a vision.
THE POSSESSED falls to the ground, writhing in a seizure, then leaps
about toward others on stage, then falls again, etc.]

THE POSSESSED
The pineapple... 34!

ENSEMBLE MEN
Shake not the head!
Shake not the feet!

Shake not the legs!

Roll not the eyes!
Don't lift one eyebrow
Higher than the other!

Bedew no man's face
With your spittle!

[WASHINGTON THE BOY produces a pine cone]

THE POSSESSED
The pine cone... 34!

ENSEMBLE MEN
Shake not the head!
Shake not the feet!
Shake not the legs!

Roll not the eyes!
Don't lift one eyebrow
Higher than the other!

Bedew no man's face
With your spittle!
ENSEMBLE WOMEN
We should put those with whom we speak before ourselves...

ENSEMBLE MEN
In the case that they be our superiors.

ENSEMBLE WOMEN
Never — 49 — use reproachful language against anyone...

ENSEMBLE MEN
When you deliver a matter to do it without passion and without discretion. 83.

ENSEMBLE WOMEN
Reproach not — rule 70 — reproach not the imperfections of others.

ENSEMBLE MEN
That belongs to parents.
To masters
And to superiors. 70.

ENSEMBLE WOMEN
67 says don't detract from others
Or be excessive —

[THE POSSESSED seizes the pineapple.
THE EXCLUDED (women and people of color)
become suddenly possessed as they grab the pineapple.]

THE EXCLUDED
50! 22! 21! 50! 22! 21! (repeats)

WASHINGTON THE MAN
Let your recreations be manful, not sinful.
Seven.

[THE EXCLUDED rise]

THE EXCLUDED
Don't believe rumors
Rumors
Rumors
Don't believe

THE EMPOWERED
Superfluous comments are to be avoided.

[THE EMPOWERED and THE EXCLUDED
dance the Double-Face Tango]

THE EXCLUDED
Don't be glad

THE EMPOWERED
Don't appear

THE EXCLUDED
Don't be glad

THE EMPOWERED
Don't appear

THE EXCLUDED
Don't appear

THE EMPOWERED
To be glad

THE EXCLUDED
At your enemy's

THE EMPOWERED
Appear to be

THE EXCLUDED
Glad at your enemy's

THE EMPOWERED
Misfortune
Misfortune
Misfortune

THE EXCLUDED
21! 22! 50! 21! 22! 50!

[The limbs of THE EXCLUDED begin to explode]

THE EMPOWERED
Don't argue with your superiors. Forty.

WASHINGTON THE BOY
Reproach none for the infirmities of nature!

WASHINGTON THE MAN
When you speak of God or His Attributes,
let it be seriously and with reverence.

THE POSSESSED
How is it that a few white men become convinced
that the world is improved by their control?

## Scene 4 — THE EXPEDITION

[The pulse sound heard at the opening reappears]

WASHINGTON THE MAN
If the conduct of Americans, while promoting their own happiness,
should influence the feelings of other nations

THE EXCLUDED (turning toward A)
Other nations?

THE EMPOWERED
Other nations.

WASHINGTON THE MAN
And thereby render a service to mankind,
the Americans will receive a double pleasure.

VOICE FROM ENSEMBLE
Preparing to encounter our audience. Ready to test the Rules.

[THE EMPOWERED pull THE EXCLUDED to attention.
THE ENSEMBLE, including WASHINGTON THE MAN and WASH-
INGTON THE BOY become THE EXPEDITIONARY FORCE.]

VOICES FROM THE ENSEMBLE
*77!*
Rule! *66! 30!*
Rule!
*37! 38! 39!*
Rule!
*11!*
Rule!
*47!*
Rule!
*57!*
Rule!
*89!*
Rule!
*75! 76!*
Rule!
*59!*
Rule!

28! 29!
Rule!
68!
Rule!

[THE EXPEDITIONARY FORCE descends from the stage into the house.]

ENSEMBLE
Walking... Walking... Walking

VOICE FROM ENSEMBLE
Moving from point A to point B.

VOICE FROM ENSEMBLE
Although he used Euclid's geometry as a tool, Washington never worked
through the principles. He preferred Rules.

ENSEMBLE
Rules... Rules...

[As THE EXPEDITIONARY FORCE enters foreign territory, their march
slows and becomes a Chinese Imperial Grapevine
progressing along the Paths of Left and Right]

FEMALE VOICE
In walking the highest place in most countries seems to be on the right hand...

FEMALE VOICE
So place yourself to the left of him you desire to honor

FEMALE VOICE
But if three walk together the middle place is the most honorable of all...

MALE VOICE
In walking up and down a house, with one greater than yourself,
yield the right to him...

MALE VOICE
If he be a man of great quality, walk not with him cheek by jowl...

[THE EXPEDITIONARY FORCE stops and turns toward A]

VOICE FROM ENSEMBLE
When you meet someone of greater quality than yourself, stop.

ENSEMBLE
When you meet someone of greater quality than yourself, stop.

[EF approaches members of A]

ENSEMBLE
Go not thither, where you know not whether you'll be welcome... welcome...
welcome... whether you'll be welcome or not.

WASHINGTON THE BOY
If anyone comes to speak to you while you are sitting, stand up.

[EF gets individual members of the audience — their personal
"A-contact" — to stand]

ENSEMBLE
If anyone comes to speak to you while you are sitting, stand up.

WASHINGTON THE MAN
Give to every person his due title according to his degree,

[THE EXPEDITIONARY FORCE interviews A to determine their degree
and then gives them their title. Using words, each person makes her/his
inquiry in a different way — i.e., one person may look for signs of friendship
and then name the A contact, "Friend," another may ask background
questions and name their A contact, "Bachelor of Arts,"
or "Venus," or "Unemployed," etc.]

[Once the A contacts are titled, the EF begins to examine them
for signs of illness]

DIRECTOR
Don't play the physician if you don't know anything about it.

DIRECTOR
Be not forward, but kindly and courteous.

DIRECTOR
In speaking to people of quality, do not look at them full in the face.

DIRECTOR
When you are talking, don't point with your finger at another's face.

DIRECTOR
Don't mock or joke about anything important. Don't make sharp, biting jokes.

DIRECTOR
Never express anything unbecoming.

## Scene 5 — THE INSURRECTION

THE EXCLUDED
Don't speak of death or wounds
Or melancholy things
Change the discourse
If you can
[THE EXCLUDED begin to confer in secret with the A. They move through the aisles through secret biomechanical signals to each other and the A. THE EMPOWERED hurl themselves from the back of the stage toward the A when they speak, but are thrown back by the secret signals of the excluded.]

THE EXCLUDED (whispering)
Rule 60:
Don't be immodest in urging your friends to discover a secret.

THE EMPOWERED
Be as courteous as a person's rank demands. It is absurd to act the same with a clown and a prince. 42.
THE EXCLUDED
18. Don't read another's books or writings unless asked to.

THE EMPOWERED
89. Don't speak evil of the absent. It is unjust.

THE EXCLUDED
Don't identify your sources. 79.

THE EMPOWERED
Don't disturb the audience. 74.

THE EXCLUDED
Don't approach those that speak in private. 81.

[THE EXCLUDED secure a Promise
from their contacts to take action at a secret signal]

THE EMPOWERED
Don't speak in unknown tongues. 72.

[THE EMPOWERED establish their Court on stage. THE EXCLUDED
occupy the stairs/ramps to the house. Each exchange is a physical Trial.]

THE EXCLUDED
Don't pretend to teach your equals. 41.

THE EMPOWERED
Let your conversation be without malice or envy. 58.

THE EXCLUDED
Be blameless of what you accuse another. 48.

THE EMPOWERED
Don't argue with your superiors. 40.

THE EXCLUDED
Consider whether you should speak publicly or privately. 45.

THE EMPOWERED
Don't be so eager to win that you overstep your bounds.

[THE EMPOWERED overwhelm THE EXCLUDED.

THE EXCLUDED move to escape and take off
through the aisles in a rebellious Liberation Dance.]

THE EMPOWERED
53! 53! 53!
Don't run in the streets.
Don't shake your arms.
Don't kick the ground.
Don't move on your toes in a dancing fashion.

[THE EMPOWERED overtake THE EXCLUDED in the house.
They remove their ties and sashes, turn them inside out and
spread the camouflage combat cloth over THE EXCLUDED.]

THE EMPOWERED
Submit to the judgment of the majority. 86.


### Scene 6 — THE PUNISHMENT

[The fearful light and sounds of war. A phantasm of punishments. Food as flesh. Drink as blood. As the punishments are enacted around the theater, WASHINGTON THE BOY and WASHINGTON THE MAN sit down at center stage, carve up the pineapple and eat it.]

VOICES FROM THE ENSEMBLE
Obedience to the rules is a necessary condition of war.
What is the difference between the rules of civility and the rules of war?
The rules of civility govern how we appear.
The rules of war govern what we do.

At times the rules are prayers for peace.
We pray in the language we are taught.

MALE VOICE
Don't sit at the head of the table, unless it is your proper place,
unless it is your proper place.

FEMALE VOICE
Or the master of the house wishes it. Or the master of the house wishes it.

MALE VOICE
It is the decent thing to do to give anyone at table a meal.
FEMALE VOICE
Try to help others.

DUET
Unless your master desires it not.

WASHINGTON THE BOY
In my time, the pineapple stood for the sweet riches of colonial conquest.

WASHINGTON THE MAN
It is the place of the most important in the company to unfold his napkin and begin eating first. Therefore he ought to begin on time and do it efficiently so that the slowest may have enough time. [Punishment Music]

FEMALE VOICE
Pay attention when others talk at the table.

DUET
Don't lay your arm but only your hand on the table.

FEMALE VOICE
Keep your fingers clean and when they're dirty wipe them on a napkin.

WASHINGTON THE MAN
When in the company of your betters, don't be longer in eating than they are.
Also, it is no longer customary to drink to others every time you drink.
[Punishment Music]

MALE VOICE
Don't eat in the streets or in the house out of season!

FEMALE VOICE
Don't drink too leisurely or too hastily!

DUET
Don't spit, don't scratch, don't cough or blow your nose. Except when really
necessary! Don't cut your bread with a greasy knife.

WASHINGTON THE MAN
It's unbecoming to stoop over one's food or make noise when you breathe.
It's uncivil! [Punishment Music]

FEMALE VOICE
Don't put your food in your mouth with a knife!!

MALE VOICE
Don't eat pieces too big for your mouth!!

FEMALE VOICE
Don't put another bite of food until the first one is finished!!

MALE VOICE
Don't stare while you are drinking!!

DUET
And don't talk when your mouth is full!!

WASHINGTON THE MAN
Don't make a show of delighting in your food! Or eat too greedily!
Don't find fault with what you eat!!!
[Punishment Music]

DUET
Don't get angry at the table whatever happens. Put on a cheerful face,
especially if there are strangers present.
Good humor makes one dish of food a feast!!!

WASHINGTON THE MAN
Don't clean your teeth with a knife. If others do it... use a toothpick.
[Punishment Music]

THE EXCLUDED
Break the rules!
Remove the mask of war!
Pull!

## Scene 7 — THE ENTHRONEMENT

VOICE FROM THE ENSEMBLE
The icon of George Washington is a fundamental pillar of American culture.
The Rules have yet to be finally decoded.

WASHINGTON THE MAN
These are the things which once possessed
Will make a life that's truly blessed
A good estate on healthy soil
Not got by vice, nor yet by toil
Round a warm fire, a pleasant joke
With chimney ever free from smoke
A strength entire, a sparkling bowl
A quiet wife, a quiet soul
A merry night without much drinking
A happy thought without much thinking

VOICE FROM ENSEMBLE
When you sit down, keep your feet firm and even,
without putting one on the other or crossing them.

VOICE FROM ENSEMBLE
Don't turn your back on others. Don't lean on anyone.

VOICE FROM ENSEMBLE
When a man does all he can and doesn't succeed, don't blame him.

VOICE FROM ENSEMBLE
The world is reinventing its rules of civility and decent behavior.

VOICE FROM ENSEMBLE
It's better to be alone than in bad company.

VOICE FROM ENSEMBLE
A man ought not to value himself for his achievements, or rare quality of wit;
much less for his virtue, his relatives or his riches.

VOICE FROM ENSEMBLE
Don't make comparisons!

VOICE FROM ENSEMBLE
The new rules of civility and decent behavior are rules
that cannot be imposed.

VOICE FROM ENSEMBLE
Carry yourself in a manner becoming a serious, settled person.
Don't contradict what others say.

VOICE FROM ENSEMBLE
Don't repeat the same thing often.
ENSEMBLE
No more war... No more war...

WASHINGTON THE BOY
Work at keeping alive in your heart that little spark
of celestial fire called conscience.

ENSEMBLE
No more war... No more war...

[EPILOG]

Fig. 18
*Waste*: Performing on Third Street   *[Photo: Gianfranco Mantegna]*

# 7
# WASTE

Waste was chosen as the theme for our next street theater project. In our group discussions, the company repeatedly came around to a strong desire to address environmental issues. Looking at the panoply of such concerns, I was struck by the way in which all kinds of resource mismanagement stem from a wasteful approach to the global situation. Moreover, there is a revolutionary implication inherent in the concept of waste: there can be waste only where it would be possible to do otherwise and waste not.

I adopted a kind of "March of Drama" approach, lifting scenes from their settings along the timetrack of theater history from the Greeks to Robert Wilson, and presenting them pageant-like in the street in chronological order. The preface to the script explains:

> *Waste* is an outdoor spectacle performed on warm evenings in parks, vacant lots and closed-off streets. The play presents a wide array of societal problems plaguing us in the current era, all of them examples of wastefulness — pollution, famine, homelessness, crime and war among them. Industrial and domestic waste products poison the air and water. The despair of wasted lives leads to desperate acts.

I determined to create a script on this basis. Judith would direct.

Human lives are extinguished by hunger and malnutrition despite the existence of abundant food reserves. People unable to cope with the system are left to waste away — the unemployed suffocate in their private misery, the homeless decay in public, the imprisoned rot hidden away in jail. Wars continue ceaselessly in one part of the world or another, wasting entire peoples and their achievements. The diversity of species dwindles. Fossil fuels and nuclear fission are employed to generate power at enormous expense to the environment while clean energy is neglected. Waste, waste, waste.

Yet the notion of waste has a positive side. It seems to contain within it the seeds of alternatives. If our approach to a given situation appears wasteful, it would follow that other, less improvident approaches are possible. In its way, *Waste* is an example of Brecht's concept of an epic theater. In his "Little Organon for the Theater" Brecht writes that the spectator in the traditional theater, identifying with the protagonist, is moved by his sufferings because they appear inevitable, whereas the spectator in the epic theater is moved because the character's sufferings are revealed to be unnecessary. That is, wasteful.

This is the idea behind *Waste*. The actors encourage the audience to assist them in acting out the ways in which we lay waste to our lives and the planet and invite them to explore solutions. They distribute a peace proposal from the War Resisters League and an invitation to an I.W.W. forum on revolutionary unionism. Most importantly, the actors encourage the audience to imagine non-wasteful ways of getting along in the world, a necessary first step toward implementing them.

To create the text, I ransacked the various canons of dramatic literature, gleaning a broad range of theatrical forms from among the masterpieces of various genres. Aeschylus' Thebans challenging fate become New Yorkers contesting their city's tragic destiny. The *commedia dell'arte* story of Flavio's quest for the hand of Flaminia turns on a trick of agribusiness instead of on a trick of disguise. In the medieval *Harrowing of Hell*, the Master of the Chester Cycle has Jesus free the Old Testament crew from Satan's grasp; in *Waste*, Jesus rescues the homeless and imprisoned. Zeami's N-play traveller dreams, not about the glory of the Imperial throne, but about the glory of unpolluted water. Hamlet visits the Indian Point Nuclear Power plant and broods over questions of its safety. Sardou's *Scrap of Paper* is transformed into a mountain of garbage which, as in the 19th-century farce, must be concealed at all costs.

*Tosca's* Cavaradossi paints his vision of the hidden harmony of species diversity rather than that of blondes and brunettes. Mother Courage not only tells the soldiers that war dooms them, as in Brecht's play, but she and Catherine proceed to disarm them. The trio of David Mamet's *American Buffalo* are rescued from despair by the I.W.W. Finally, Robert Wilson's *Einstein on the Beach* converges with The Living Theatre's *Waste* project as an ecstatic vision of new power and energy arrangements.

Each genre was chosen as an embodiment of some aspect of our thematic concerns in *Waste*. Thus Greek tragedy seems a likely source for a scene about attitudes toward destiny, French comedy for a scene about keeping something out of sight, the Japanese Noh drama for one about the quest for purity, and so on. In every case the original is a brilliant landmark in theatrical history and I have tried to preserve some quintessential feeling of the original author's genius in each. But I have also been shameless in discarding everything in the original which is irrelevant to the theme of *Waste*, and substituting all manner of words and actions to accomplish our own purpose.

Because the performances of *Waste* are all to take place in public spaces and no money is involved (no one pays, no one is paid), I have not troubled to ask permission of the surviving sources of our literary inspiration. I trust that they would approve of this public-spirited, non-commercial use of their work.

Malina breathed theatrical life into the production by devising a staging plan based on alternating scenes between two stages erected at opposite ends of the space, the audience grouped between. Lights were hung on towers at the four corners. Thanks to a municipal grant of sound equipment, microphones were suspended by wires above the entire playing area. We obtained permits to close off streets and were given access to electrical power from city lampposts.

Despite the weightiness of the social problem in view, the parodistic element of the play's concept infused the entire performance with a comic light-heartedness which balanced the evening so well that audiences responded with delight. Even *New York Times* critic Don Bruckner was disarmed enough to express in print considerable enthusiasm for the work. During the first summer that we performed *Waste*, in 1991, we transformed the Third Street theater and lobby into a "Waste Museum" where artists from the community were invited to display and perform works on the theme of waste. The Waste Museum's painting and sculpture exhibitions, play, poetry and fiction readings, music and dance concerts, and performance events were much frequented by local residents. It became a beehive of activity that spilled paint, music, and all manner of creative ferment right out of the storefront and onto the sidewalk.

As for the play proper, we were so well-satisfied with its effect on audiences, and especially those in our backyard, that we decided to give the play another full series of performances around town the following summer. Here are a few performance memories that might give a sense of the event:

— Droves of Lower East Side toddlers mustered into the army during the *Mother Courage* scene, marching toward revolt with their rolled-newspaper rifles on their shoulders.

—The Union Square performance, where Maria Piscator was so overwhelmed by the Total Theater quality of the work that she would not go home without first writing a sizeable check. And Bernard Goetz appeared, too, that night, like a spectre among the audience. Afterwards, he paused to speak with us of his enthusiasm for our anti-establishmentarianism, and of his skepticism about our utopian aspirations.

— The East Seventh Street Recycling Center performance where the journalist from the *Village Voice* had an authentic, unrehearsed rat leap across her seated-on-the-ground body during the play. She wrote a nasty review. Curiously, throughout our tenure at Third Street, the *Voice* rarely voiced anything but displeasure with our efforts, whereas the *Times* was nearly always guardedly positive.

— Jerry's waggish Einstein, Alan's holier-than-thou Jesus, Gene's lustful Devil, Bob Paton's visionary dreamer, Laura's cough-racked Queen Victoria, Marlene's garbage-wary Suzanne, Bobby's globe-juggling Cavaradossi, and, of course, the "Wastettes" (as ensemble stalwarts Isha, Emily, Lauren, Kristin, Nadia, Deena, and others came to call themselves) rearranging the plexiglas prison bars of hell into a heavenly geodesic polyhedron (Garrick Beck taught us that trick).

— Nonstop harassment by the police throughout the Washington Square performance, despite our official permit.

— And the rains came... as at the East River Park performance that dissolved in a thunderstorm that had us scampering through diluvial sheets of water trying to rescue the artfully-strung sound equipment from extinction as lightning bolts crashed down around us. Some of the actor/technicians took all their clothes off in celebration of the sheer extremity of the situation. And the performance at La Plaza Cultural, where a throng of the faithful waited under plastic sheets for the rain to stop for what seemed like hours and were rewarded with a particularly passionate performance. And at the playground at 99th Street and AmsterdamAvenue where the rain simply wouldn't stop and we said well, then, no... and all crawled away, feeling like faithless rats.

— At performance after performance, an heroic company drawing prodigious strength in the street directly from the community, becoming part of the community in the playing.

## Excerpt from Judith Malina's Diary

August 2, 1991

How lovely is this site! All the problems fall away as a few spectators gather at the gate...

About a hundred people come. Neighborhood people and artists. They sit on the glass-strewn ground, some bring plastic bags to sit on. Most sit on the great manure piles, that are at least soft and full of excess glass shards, but have their own quality. Garrick and Tameron [Beck], Pamela Badyk and Steve Ben Israel, Eva Brenner....

Steve sits beside me. I often run from one side of the playing space to the other, or to the sound, run by Patrick Grant, or to the lights run bravely by Nicola Marchetti, or to Michael Shenker.... But mostly, I watch admiringly as the epic unrolls....

And the guys from the notorious laundromat and the dealers from the street watch the play, which begins in the late daylight, but enters darkness before the Noh play pilgrims go out in search of water....

The prologue is long, but the audience is responsive enough to support the workshops, and the singing of solidarity forever, which has a fine ring in the Loisaida night.

The opening speeches of Gary Brackett and Jerry Goralnick, the brothers Eteocles and Polyneikes as campaigning politicians, set the classical, political tone.... The women of the Chorus, eloquent on their three garbage pails, evoke the anachronism, modern/ancient. Then Alan Arenius runs in with news — a glimmer of our future.... By the time the first scene with its lyric tone begins, the audience is warmly involved — children everywhere, the young men joshing, the women, wide-eyed.

The second scene is the Commedia: Our Vegetarian Entry/Entree. Oats, peas, beans, and barley grow, as the ensemble performs our version of the Agricultural Movement.... Bob Paton is coyly stylized as Pantalone, trying to marry his daughter off to his rich old friend Dr. Grantiano. Alan Arenius, ever versatile, plays the ugly doctor with gusto. Johnson Anthony plays an Arlecchina that is almost painfully servile, acrobatic, and with a high, crazy voice. I fear now that his portrayal may be regarded as racist. It hadn't occurred to me — in a kind of color-blind casting — that in front of an audience, which may not be color-blind, the black Harlequin is being beaten up by a white Gratiano and Pantalone.

Our audience is amused at the tricks and tempo of the style, as we imitate them. Johnson's particularly good at the shenanigans, his circus background an advantage in the many prat falls and tumbles.... It recalls the root of street theatre: the bare platform, the sharp, tough acting style — Jerry is quite Agit-Prop about the vegetables... and he looks the image of a commedia actor, or maybe, something Watteau.

The shameless exhortation to vegetarianism is well taken by this audience. They sing along with the ditty, "For you and I and everyone know that eating meat has got to go!"

❀❀❀❀❀❀❀❀

Then the dramatic swivel from the bare-bone speech and rambling raving derived from Mamet, to the austere formality of the Noh play... the Mother Courage marching goes on and on, too long.

An audience member with a paper gun, staggering drunk, who had been marching all along during the Noh and the Mamet plays, now gets in everyone's way. Mother Courage's wagon frame falls backward and there's a visible confusion behind the little stage.... I rush over there, as does Hanon. From the other side we see the children, who have been sort of charmingly underfoot until now, make off with the shovels. Actually, I'm surprised at how little went wrong, everything being so fragile and under-rehearsed.

# 8
# THE ZERO METHOD

This is a play meant to clear the slate. To lay our cards on a *tabula rasa*. A play in which Malina and I, responsible for guiding the great ship of The Living Theatre past the shoals of historical irrelevancy toward the golden shore of communion with the contemporary audience, are alone on stage, confronting the void. We tell our own story, how the two of us first came into contact at a performance of *Mysteries and smaller pieces* at Yale in 1968 and we relate in theatrical enactment everything from that moment forward to the existential crisis here and now in the theater. As the play takes an essentially empirical approach to our experience, it seemed that the structural elements of such reasoning could be brought into full view by staking our experience to the seven step ontological approach of Wittgenstein's *Tractatus Logico-Philosophicus*. I wrote a text interweaving a philosophical dialogue between ourselves with audience encounters, leavening Wittgenstein's austere exactitudes with original poetry and a fleeting citation from Rilke. The play attempts to "take it to zero," to question the theatrical act itself, turning up the house lights in the middle of play and asking the public directly, "What sort of basis is there for our relationship, exactly?" We felt ourselves like Cretan bull leapers, taking the would-be-spectators by the horns as we talked directly with them about the harsh reality of the company's situation, asking them to address their own responsibilities in the matter of economic support for the arts here and now in this theater. We never did go so far as to actually collect money, for fear of poisoning the purity of the philosophical inquiry. Besides, most of them had paid a small sum for their ticket.

The play begins and ends with a rope. A kind of umbilicus up which we climb out of the subterranean dressing room into the world. And the play ends with a tug-of-war between J and H which resolves in a joyous balancing act. Such, the play concludes, is love. Between these points, we two trace a path as Wittgensteinian detectives in private-eye garb, sweeping up the aisles as we search the house for clues, tricked-out "disguises" (and magnifying glass in hand). Time and again, we shed the trench coat, fedora, and dark glasses to address the real work of formulating the propositions which seem the only means of making sense of our lives. The detective episodes and the *Tractatus* passages alternate on the one hand with recollections of a series of luminous details from the tapestry of our years together, and on the other, with the crucial encounters wherein we enjoin the audience to enrich the play's content themselves, i.e., participate creatively.

For example, after a lively polling scene that always delighted the crowd ("How many of you like the play so far? Raise your hands." etc.), I navigated the aisles with a hand-held microphone, soliciting direct responses to our concerns from the audience. This put us in a vulnerable situation. One night Laurie Anderson passed the microphone to her German-accented companion, who took the occasion to complain that he found the play boring. Often, however, an attack from one quarter of the house inspired another to passionate defense. When that happened, we were more than happy to let them fight it out between themselves — we were home free and tried not to smile too smugly.

*The Zero Method* called for an ur-simple set in unequivocal primary colors. I suggested an open stage space in which appears a hard-surfaced yellow cube about a yard long on each side and a slightly larger soft-surfaced blue rectangular form. At the back of the stage, I had thought to install a red rectangle, but Ilion brought the idea elegantly into being with the aid of Gary, who brilliantly transformed the upstage screen into two overlapping irregular red cloths stretched tight in spiky curves like two nerve cells at synapse.

Patrick Grant contributed a spare, lucid tape and synthesizer score that was remarkable for its eloquent silences. The correlation between the progression of the *Tractatus* theses (*italics*) and biographical events is outlined in the play's program as follows:

ACT 1
*The world is all that is the case.*
They are born, they discover the world, themselves, each other.

ACT 2
*What is the case — a fact — is the existence of states of affairs.*
They become lovers inside a complicated preexisting situation.

ACT 3
*A logical picture of facts is a thought.*
They marry.

ACT 4
*A thought is a proposition with a sense.*
They make a life for themselves.

ACT 5
*A proposition is a truth-function of elementary propositions.*
They struggle with the world's opposition.

## ACT 6
*Every proposition is a result of successive applications*
*to elementary propositions of an operation.*
They adopt a procedure.

## ACT 7
*That of which we cannot speak we must pass over in silence.*
They confront their own demise.

We did two runs of *The Zero Method* at Third Street, at the end of 1991, before touring the play in Italy in early 1992, and again toward the end of that year. Edoardo Fadini, a critic and presenter of *il Living* in Torino since their first visit in the 1960's, organized tour after tour for us. He was the first of the Italian intellectuals to champion the new, post-Julian work with real enthusiasm. "*È bestiale!*" he exclaimed, beaming, after seeing *Il Metodo Zero* for the first time.

The play was important to us on several levels. It was another exploratory venture into the world of nonfictional theater, both in terms of the work's autobiographical content, and its insistence on direct dialogue with the audience. It was also a rare insistence of our actually translating into theatrical action the essential postulates of a philosophical work as airily conceptual as Wittgenstein's *Tractatus*.

Equally, it was an occasion to share with the public the flavor of a trans-generational love affair surviving across time. And finally, touring in Europe with a small cast produced enough revenue to keep the operation on Third Street going for many months.

Figs. 19 and 20
*Zero Method*: Hanon Reznikov, above; Judith Malina and Hanon
Reznikov, below *[Photos: Ira Cohen, above, and Bill Leissner, below]*

# THE ZERO METHOD

by Hanon Reznikov

THE LIVING THEATRE
December, 1991

## ACT 1

[H and S appear climbing up a rope out of the darkness. When they arrive inside the theater space, they spray-paint the letter "A" inside a circle on the wall. Blackout. H and S then appear in various parts of the theater, singly and together, committing crimes between blackouts. First, H steals a diamond necklace from S. Then, H and S are seen setting a fire.
Finally, H strangles S, who then screams during the final blackout.
Lights up on Wittgenstein (H dressed in detective garb: trench-coat, fedora and sunglasses) standing over S's body.]

WITTGENSTEIN
The world is all that is the case.

SHE
[rising] Oh, Wittgenstein, is this your first thesis, or what?

WITTGENSTEIN
The world is the totality of facts, not of things.

SHE
But why are you dressed as a detective?

WITTGENSTEIN
I am conducting an investigation. You are all suspects. So am I, of course. Besides, I lived in England many years. I always liked very much the clothes.

SHE
But much time has passed since then. You've been dead.

WITTGENSTEIN

We cannot speak of "the passage of time" — there is no such thing —
we can speak only of the movement of the hands of the chronometer)....
The world, however, is determined by the facts, and by their being all the
facts. Consequently, the totality of facts determines what is the case,
and also whatever is not the case.

SHE

It's as if you wanted me to pretend to listen to this,
in order to make the audience hear it.

WITTGENSTEIN

That is part of what needs to happen.

SHE

But is this a method of some kind?

WITTGENSTEIN

You could call it a zero-method. [exits]

SHE

The facts, then, as we know them, define some kind of space. And this space
is, in fact, the world. [to audience] But how does this answer to your needs?

HE

[enters from rear of house] I see what the audience wants. They want it to be
beautiful, but ice-clear and distant as a star. They want to experience accelera-
tion, the rush of blood and hormones that aesthetic engineering can deliver.

SHE

They want to love us and feel that we love them, individually and uncondi-
tionally. They would like to be let off the hook. They want to be at the beach;
if we could meet them there, we might find them favorably disposed.

HE

They want to be surprised, but only pleasantly. If we propose to approach
them, they would prefer that we do not come from behind. If we were to invite them to come toward us, they would need to see a comfortable spot in our
direction in order to be moved to change their arrangements.

SHE

They would like our voices to be sharp and expressive. They would be re-
lieved if we used no political words, or if at the very least, we framed the polit-

ical words with historical rubber bumpers — they like it when I talk about "what we used to call the revolution." They would like to see us naked if our bodies were youthful, but they would prefer not to see us naked when our bodies are old. Something to do with death.

HE

They're longing desperately for encouragement, to be able to feel that the endless exertions, both physical and emotional, which life demands of them are somehow worth the effort. They would like us to be aware of how hard they try. They would like to be forgiven for not trying hard enough.

SHE

They would leap with excitement if the ordinary were made to seem glorious by having lurid colored lights thrown on it, especially if accompanied by mysterious music. They would like to be approached sexually, but only in a way they have never experienced before.

[S and H embrace sensually]

SHE

I know exactly what I want from them.

HE

I want them to smile from ear to ear.

SHE

I would be pleased to move them to tears, the tears that accompany the reunion of the alienated self with its long-lost other half. I want them to take hold of the strength and power of that reunion and use it to deepen their commitment.

HE

I would like them to wake as from a dream and to understand for the first time whatever it is that they have been needing to understand. I would like this understanding to proceed from a rational process, but I also know that sometimes the greatest moral force in art is felt when you suddenly feel like your shoes are brand new on your feet.

SHE

I would like the best among them to leave addresses and telephone numbers.

HE

Is this an elementary proposition?

SHE
Is this an operation?

[light change]

SHE
One

HE
I was in college when I first saw her.

SHE
One dollar

HE
She was reciting the Brig Dollar Poem onstage
in *Mysteries and smaller pieces* when the company opened at Yale in 1968.

SHE
This certifies that there is

HE
That piercing clarity in her voice. "Malina," I thought,
looking at the program, "maybe she's Latin American."

SHE
On deposit in the treasury

HE
I began to imagine her as a kind of Peruvian sorceress.

SHE
Of the United States

HE
I was born in the United States.

SHE
The United States of America.

HE
I was born in 1950.

SHE

I was born first. [H exits] I have no homeland, nor have I lost one;
my mother simply let me out of her body and into the world. It happened
in Germany in a city called Kiel, sixty-five years ago. I think I remember
gulls and trolley wires in front of the sky, but I left early in my life
and travelled far and I have travelled further since.
Here and now I stand in the world at [The Living Theatre on Third Street]
at [9pm], moving with you now deeper into the world, and I have faith in you
and I have doubts about you and both of these are mine.
And yet history holds me hostage. I'm a woman with a past whose theater
family blossomed in color and spread to factory and field and grew weary
of its own legend and was already far too old; — and what they left me
and what I gained of art and protest is homeless.
In my hands, in my round belly I have to hold it all, until I die.
Since nothing I put away out into the world falls, but rises upon a wave,
independent of my will.

WITTGENSTEIN

[enters] We are not yet ready to consider the nature of the will. That will
come later, as a corollary of the sixth thesis. In any case, what is significant at
this point is that the world divides into facts.

SHE

Yes, Wittgenstein, but any one fact can either be the case or not be the case,
and everything else remain the same. [light change]

## ACT 2

HE

In the second of the seven thematic steps of his Tractatus, Wittgenstein says
that what is the case — a fact — is a combination of things.

SHE

Each fact, however, specifies a different combination of things.

HE

For us personally, it was a matter of becoming lovers inside a complicated
preexisting situation.

SHE

In this, as in other things, the important thing is to establish a method.

WITTGENSTEIN (tape)
Just as we cannot think of spatial objects at all apart from space,
or temporal objects apart from time, so we cannot think of any object apart
from the possibility of its connection with other things.

[H and S begin enactments of Epic Theater: a series of biomechanical études
based on actions developed for *The Legacy of Cain* cycle of street play.]

HE
We were some crazy combinations. Chanting down the street
with the campesinos dressed in purple and green
in support of the grape and lettuce boycott.

SHE
You built me a tower in our backyard in Brooklyn
and I loved you from the window.

HE
We were Julian Beck in revolt against his parents
and the complacency of the entire bourgeoisie.

SHE
We were making inroads with the poorest of the poor.

HE
We were Judith Malina keeping to a revolutionary schedule.

SHE [stopping enactments]
I am keeping to a revolutionary schedule. It is you who are late.

HE
Yes, but it is also I who have written these lines.

SHE
And the company?

HE
They're not here now. It's just us.

SHE [indicates audience]
What about them?

HE

From here they are dim forms. Their eyes are invisible.
It is impossible to know what they are thinking.

SHE

It is hard to speak to one another as if they were not there.

HE

It is harder to speak to them directly. We don't know who they are.

SHE

And the company?

HE

As I said, they're not here now. It's just us.

SHE

I don't like it. I feel... lessened.

HE

Then I'm not doing a good enough job as a husband.

SHE

Oh, please! Don't even start with that. Don't you know how much
the audience wants to see The Living Theatre as a group presence?

HE

I don't think we should necessarily be doing
what the audience wants us to do —

SHE

No, I don't either. But don't you see how much more fully
we could communicate our experience if the company were here
to enact the world around us.

HE

I can do that. So can you. We've been doing it already. You go on and tell
them about finding each other and I'll be the ensemble bringing the story
to life. I'm always willing to take on a lot. The first time I performed was
in kindergarten — the girl playing the Big Bad Wolf got stage fright when
the mothers arrived for the show and I rushed up to the teacher and said,
"Mrs. Gutstein, I know the lines! I can do it!'

SHE
He is, if anything, overconfident.

HE
It's a good strategy for as long as you can get away with it.
Go ahead, tell them what it was like twenty years ago when we met.
On what basis did we decide to take up with one another?

WITTGENSTEIN (tape)
Objects contain the possibility of all states of affairs.

SHE
[biomechanical enactments resume — H enacts The Knight's Arrival]
You are the foreign prince
Who never came to Aquitaine
To ease Eleanor's sorrow over Henry
And plant peace among the mucky brood.
[H enacts People's Street Theater]
I woke in the night hearing shouts, seeing
Banners — my theater was in the streets.
You threw your body headlong into
The biomechanical mass, face
Into asphalt, blood onto walls,
Every action a public act —
There were arrests but no denials.
[H enacts Love Grapes]
Something of you — your height, your boots —
Broke me off from the trunk of habit,
Grafted me to a supple vine
Through which joy
Flashed like juice into grapes.

[H enacts Travel Arrangements]
In Pittsburgh, Rio, New York and Prague,
Vienna, Barcelona, Dublin, Seville,
Portugal, Poland, Paris, Helsinki,
LA, Mycenae, Rome and Berlin —
In so many places that memory chokes
On the rich-layered life we still lead,
We folded into the recesses of each others' lives
Like telepathic twins.
[H and S approach each other slowly]
And now everything is different,

Temporary and final, things happen,
But never quite of their own. For something
Has given my poor warm life
Into the hand of a Russian seer
Who looks in my eyes and tells me
What it is that yesterday I was.

HE
In saying what she said she said all that she said and she said that
she did say what she said when she was saying what she said, and
she said that she said what she said in saying what she said and she
was saying what she said when she said what she said.

SHE
The picture, however, represents what it represents, independently of its truth
or falsehood, through the form of representation.

HE
On the other hand, in order to discover whether the picture is true or false
we must compare it with reality.
[house lights on]

SHE [to audience]
Reality. That's you.

HE
We are here, performing this play about our lives and the theater. In part we
appear here before you because, in Wittgenstein's words,

WITTGENSTEIN (tape)
Substance is what exists independently of what is the case.

SHE
And it is as substance that we appear in your visual field.
And it is as substance that we push our voices into your ears.

HE
And it is as substance that we touch you. I can understand how many
of you might prefer to see us run up the aisles naked with chain saws.

SHE
But we're just not going to do that.

HE
Instead, we're going to pursue the next of the propositions.

SHE
Namely, that the form is the possibility of the structure.

HE
Now if by the theatrical form, we can achieve some kind of consensus
among the people here, then we will have a living illustration not only
of this philosophical proposition, but also of an anarchist principle.

SHE
I think it would be a good idea while it's still early in the play,
to settle accounts about why we're here.

HE
Why we're here, and why you're here.

SHE
How many of you are here because this is a Living Theatre production?
[S and H urge audience to raise their hands in response]

HE
How many of you are here because Judith Malina is appearing in the play?

SHE
How many of you are hear because somebody bought you a ticket?

HE
Is there anybody here who came because they heard that the play
has something to do with Wittgenstein?

SHE
How many of you are more or less satisfied with how the play is going so far?

HE
Would any of you prefer that we told the story of our lives
in a more direct, narrative way?

SHE
Would any of you prefer that we spoke less and concentrated
more on sound and movement?

HE
Does anybody here wish we would stop bothering the audience
and do our job on the stage?

SHE
Is there anybody in the audience who is being paid to be here?

HE
Is there anybody who's here because
they just couldn't think of anything better to do?

SHE
Is there anybody who's here because
they're sleeping with somebody in The Living Theatre Company?

HE
The Living Theatre will gross about $200 from tonight's performance.
Does anybody here think that's enough?

SHE
Do you think that theater ought to be subsidized by the government?

HE
Do you think that an artist who is economically dependent on the government
can work freely? Let's find out where we stand on these issues.

SHE
But let's start at the beginning. Why are you here tonight?
[ad lib discussion with audience
on the relationship between performers, spectators and money —
discussion continues until consensus point is reached]

HE
The totality of propositions is the world!

SHE
A difficult and complex territory!

HE
That conspires to keep us apart!

## ACT 3

SHE
We were doing a benefit tour of *Antigone* with Amnesty International in
France many years ago and Hanon and I took off from our hotel near Orléans
early one morning and made our way to the château at Chambord. There is a
pair of spiralling stairways there, one hidden inside the other. We started
down opposite paths and could not find each other.
[during the three tellings of losing one another, H and J move in shifting arcs
about the stage, repeatedly just missing catching sight of each other]

HE
Where are you?

SHE
I'm over here.

HE
I hear you but I can't see you.

SHE
Where are you?

WITTGENSTEIN (tape)
The logical scaffolding round the picture determines the logical space.

HE
Another incident of a similar sort happened again in France in Lourdes.
We took a cable car up to a mountaintop station overlooking the Pyrenees
valley and were separated accidentally by a sudden, dense fog
as the daylight began to fade.

SHE
Hanon... Hanon!

HE
I'm here!

SHE
I can't see you...

HE
Where are you?

SHE
Hanon... Hanon!

WITTGENSTEIN (tape)
The name cannot be analyzed further by any definition.

SHE
And again, years later in a parking structure in Santa Monica,
we lost each other in interlocking stairways, and couldn't solve the mystery
of each other's wherabouts for what seemed like a long time.

HE
Malina... Malina!

SHE
Where are you?

HE
Where are you?

SHE
I'm here!

WITTGENSTEIN (tape)
The proposition reaches through the whole logical space.

HE
What is thinkable is also possible.

SHE
We got married.

HE
For the scene about the wedding, we have chosen a poem by Rilke.
[during the Rilke poem, H and S tell the story of their marriage
in the language of a modern-dance romance]

SHE
You are the bird whose wings came
when I wakened in the night and called—

HE
It is not by chance of course, that we choose Rilke.

He worked on helping Wittgenstein to get the *Tractatus* published.
In many ways they saw things eye to eye.

SHE
When I wakened in the night and called —
Only with my arms I called, because your name
is like a chasm, a thousand nights deep.

HE
For form's sake we waited three years after Julian's death,
and then we went downtown.

SHE
You are the shadows in which I quietly slept,
and each dream devised in me your seed.

HE
You are the image, but I am the frame that makes you stand in glittering relief.

SHE
We were married by a judge in the Municipal Building.

HE
What shall I call you? Look, my lips are lame.
You are the beginning that gushes forth,
I am the slow and fearful "amen"
that timidly concludes your beauty.

SHE
It was in a carpeted little secular chapel with artificial flowers —
one of those peculiar attempts to create a little bit of humanity
in the midst of the bureaucracy.

HE
Our witnesses were Mary Mary, Mark Amitin, Gianfranco Mantegna, and
Michael Smith, who designed the lighting for this production,
and who also signed our marriage certificate.

SHE
You have often snatched me out of dark rest
when sleep seemed like a grave to me
and like getting lost and fleeing, —
then you raised me out of heart-darknesses

and tried to hoist me onto all towers
like scarlet flags and bunting.

HE

It was raining that day. It was hard to know what it meant.

SHE

Something to do with hope.

HE

You: who talk of miracles as of common knowledge
and of men and women as of melodies
and of roses: of events
that in your eyes blazingly take place, —
when will you at last...
when will you at last...

SHE

A proposition can only say how a thing is, not what it is.

HE

Taking it back to the third thesis, eh? This is her way of saying,
"Don't be sentimental." All right, then.
Albania is the poorest country in Europe.

SHE
What is Albania?

HE
The poorest country in Europe.

SHE
What is the poorest country in Europe?

HE
Albania.
[H approaches S, singing "Što mi e milo"]

SHE
Are you crazy?

HE
No, I'm Albania.

SHE
Then why are you singing a Macedonian song?

HE
Is that what you have to say?

SHE
What is it we have to say?

HE
What is it I have to say?
What is it I have to say to you?
To you.
What do I think I have to say?
I have to say what I think.
Do I say what I think?
Does the thought change when spoken?

SHE
When spoken, does the thought become a proposition?

HE
What about the time?
The time.
The time between —
Between the thought and the proposition.
[very long pause — everything stops]

## ACT 4

HE
Everything that can be thought at all, can be thought clearly.

SHE
Everything that can be said, can be said clearly.

SHE & HE
We make a life for ourselves.

HE
A thought is a proposition with a sense. Thesis number four.

SHE
I make a life for myself.

HE
She makes a life for herself.

SHE
A thought is a proposition with a sense.

SHE
I make a life for myself.
I make a life for myself.
I make a life for myself.
He makes a life for himself.

HE
I make a life for myself.
I make a life for myself.
I make a life for myself.
I make a life for myself.
They make a life for themselves.
[conflictual rhythm/actions]

SHE HE
I make a life for myself. I make a life for myself.
I make a life for myself. I make a life for myself.
I make a life for myself. I make a life for myself.
I make a life for myself.

SHE
The proposition shows how things stand, but only if it is true.

HE
The proposition shows how things stand, but only if it is true?

SHE
The proposition shows how things stand, but only if it is true.
[coordinated rhythm/actions]

HE
I make a life for myself.

SHE
I make a life for myself.

HE
I make a life for myself.

SHE
We make a life for ourselves.

HE
We make a life for ourselves.

SHE & HE
We make a life for ourselves.

HE
They make a life for themselves.

SHE
By means of propositions we explain ourselves.

HE
The totality of propositions is the language.

SHE
The totality of propositions is the language!

HE
THE TOTALITY OF PROPOSITIONS IS THE LANGUAGE!

WITTGENSTEIN
What can be shown cannot be said.

SHE HE
NOT TRUE! TRUE!

SHE HE
TRUE! NOT TRUE!

**ACT 5**

HE
Zero?

SHE
Zero.

HE
How to proceed?

SHE
How to get from A to B..
.

HE
Wittgenstein's fifth thesis? Can it convince them of the basic principles?

SHE
Hard, when their inferences are all *a priori*.

HE
You mean that they're prejudiced.

SHE
I mean to complain. So many of you seem incapable of listening
to what I have to say without comparing it to what I had to say
ten or twenty or thirty or forty years ago.

HE
*The Zero Method* is the eighth play I've invented inside this company.
But few of you consider the personal quality of my work.
For most of you it's all part of some magazine story you once read
about The Living Theatre. Or even worse, a course in college.
And then there are so many misconceptions about The Living Theatre.
About the entire world. I mean, just look at the daily paper. [produces paper]
One misrepresentation after another...
Oh, look, here's your picture! [*Addams Family* theme]

SHE
No, please, not that! It's hard enough facing the fact that millions more people
will think of me forever as Granny from *The Addams Family* rather than as a
revolutionary theater artist. Give me that. [takes newspaper from H]
Listen to this. ["Kuwaitis in a Hurry to recapture the Good Life."]
[silhouette tableau]

SHE
This is about being willing to kill for money.
It isn't necessary to accept the premise at all.

HE
It doesn't have to happen.
The events of the future cannot be inferred from those of the present.
[silhouette tableau]

SHE
We were out in the streets trying to stop the Gulf War.
The war swallowed us whole. What happened? Where were you?

HE
The freedom of the will consists in the fact that you cannot know now
what you or anybody else will do in the future.

SHE
We have only three months to decide whether or not to renew our lease
on our Third Street theater.

HE
Give the money to the actors instead of to the landlord. It has a certain logic —

SHE
I want a theater.

HE
But isn't it more important to pay the actors than the landlord?

SHE
Not that our audience has proven itself capable of supporting a theater.
[silhouette tableau]

HE
I'd like you to know that this is the last self-referential play I plan to do.
From now on it's going to be about something else. History. Science.
The future. It's not going to be about me
or Judith Malina or The Living Theatre.

SHE
Of course you're wrong about that.

HE
Why do you sound like my mother?

SHE
I'm not your mother. Listen to this.
["Missouri Couple Sentenced to Die In Murder of Their Daughter, 16."]
[silhouette tableau]

SHE
They believe in punishment.

HE
And yet everything we describe could also be otherwise.
[silhouette tableau]

SHE and HE
We're sorry.

SHE
In the theater of the future nothing will seem like anything else.

HE
In the theater of the future there will be no fear of falling.

SHE
Why do you sound like a man?

HE
I am a man. Give me the paper.
Listen to this. ["Good Decade for the Rich."]
[silhouette tableau]

SHE
The news is all based on elementary propositions.
What is a "good decade?" What are "the rich?"

HE
In the theatre of the future each play will teach a new language.

SHE
Language — are we back at that?

HE
We are.
[H hands S and himself detective gear]

## ACT 6

[detective action: planting the diamond necklace stolen at the beginning
of the play on a spectator, pulling it out of her/his pocket and placing it
in a plastic evidence bag]

HE
What are we really hoping to get out of you?

SHE
Are we expecting something very different from you
than we expect from each other?

HE
How important are social conventions in this respect?
How easy is it to suspend any given rule of conduct?
For instance, if I were to touch you here... [touches audience member's arm]
I'm not really breaking any rule, am I? But if, on the other hand, I get close
to your private parts... [touches audience member's thigh]
It becomes necessary to deal with the rules. Am I going too far? If I try to
choose audience members who look like they would like me to put my hand
near their groin, I'm not likely to come up against the problem.
But if I choose somebody who might not like it at all, in order
to really lay the issue on the table, am I being authoritarian, coercive?

SHE
Let me tell you about audience participation.
On the one hand, for anarchists like us, the whole point of theater
is to point toward a model of a non-coercive society.

HE
But for the model to be sound, it needs to involve everyone actively,
including you.

SHE
But on the other hand, it is terribly difficult to get people to do more
than clap their hands or wave their arms about.
So that's what we're going to ask you to do.

HE
So, let your body sink deeper and deeper into your seat. Slide down until you
can lean your head against the back of your seat. Slide down! Now, men! All
you men in the audience — think about your mothers. Think of the thing

you'd most like to say to them but never could.
Now translate that into a movement of your arms.
Use your arms to communicate what you always wanted
to say to Mom but couldn't.
Go ahead, signal with your arms! Send those signals out!

SHE

Listen, men — you can think of me as your mother if that helps.
Send me the message again and again, until it really sinks in.

HE

Good, men! Now keep those signals going while Malina speaks.

SHE

All right, women — all the women here— think about these men acting out
their feelings toward their mothers. Look around the room and see what the
men have to say to their mothers. Now beat out an answer with your hands.
Find a code, a rhythm that says how you feel about how these men feel about
their mothers.

HE

You see how each of us is moving in a totally unique, individual way, and yet
there is a unity of purpose and effect, a collective harmony born of the free
expression of diversity. This is the whole meaning of the political process from
the point of view of anarchist aesthetics. All right, stop. The point is made.

SHE

We think this is a very oversimplified example of a very complicated social
process, but it is very hard to get the audience to do anything on the spot.

WITTGENSTEIN

In brief, by means of our willing it, the world must become quite another.
It must, so to speak, wax or wane as a whole.
But the crux of the political problem is that ethics cannot be expressed.

SHE

That's where you're wrong, Wittgenstein. Ethics is transcendental.

WITTGENSTEIN

Yes, I myself say this as a corollary of my sixth thesis, but —

SHE

This is the sixth act. Come on, everybody, back me on this one! Repeat with

me, "Ethics is transcendental." Let's say it three times together— men,
women, everyone who believes it. Ethics is transcendental.
Three times, each time stronger than the last. One!

SHE and AUDIENCE
Ethics is transcendental.

SHE
Two!

SHE and AUDIENCE
Ethics is transcendental.

SHE
Three!

SHE and AUDIENCE
Ethics is transcendental! [Blackout.]

ACT 7

HE
Is the problem as serious as Wittgenstein thought?

SHE
Oh, it's much more serious than that!
[lights: wave effect]

SHE
The earth is falling.
The house is falling.
The dogs are falling
On their snouts.
We are all falling.

HE
I am leaving.
I am leaving.
I am leaving.
I am leaving.

SHE
The glaze is on the field

And white.
The breathing is like hearing now.
Like the future.

HE [to audience]
You are now one field.
You are now one eye.
You are seeing me now
As one sees one.

SHE
He is still a child.
He is still intact.
But his blood is thin.
He bleeds,
And dies a Jew.

HE
Whereof I cannot speak —
Whereof I cannot speak —
Whereof I cannot speak —
Thereof —
[wordless interval]

SHE
I am the shore,
My eye sees it,
The wave breaks,
And it is me.
And still the gulls —
[to audience]
I am closer than before
To voices,
To pulse-beats,
To your wisdom,
To you.

HE
Whereof I cannot speak —
Whereof I cannot speak —
Whereof I cannot speak —
Thereof —
[wordless interval]

SHE
Tonight, I am gone too far out —

HE
The light goes and is not replaced.
The room darkens.

SHE
The past crowds in and disappears
Like a storm of fireflies.
I am still here.

WITTGENSTEIN (tape)
Whereof I cannot speak, thereof I must remain silent.

HE
[H throws S a life-line]
Let's be the rope!

SHE
[seizing the rope]
Let's be the rope!
[they lean toward one another and then slowly backwards,
pulling the rope taut between them — first they struggle competitively,
then they begin to work cooperatively, leaning against each other's weight
until they attain perfect balance — blackout]

## SOME HEADLINES
## INCLUDED IN *THE ZERO METHOD*
## [FROM *THE NEW YORK TIMES*]

Saturday, January 4, 1992
REBELS IN GEORGIA KILL TWO AT RALLY

FOUR ARE GIVEN MAXIMUM SENTENCES
IN UTAH TOURIST'S SUBWAY MURDER

ALGERIA SAYS ELECTION VIOLATIONS
MAY ERODE MILITANTS' ADVANTAGE

Wednesday, January 8, 1992
5 EUROPEAN OBSERVERS ARE KILLED
AS YUGOSLAV TROOPS DOWN COPTER

DEATH RATES FOR MINORITY INFANTS
WERE UNDERESTIMATED, STUDY SAYS

FURY AND PROTESTS ERUPT IN RUSSIA
AS PRICE RISES STRAIN CONSUMERS

Friday, January 10, 1992
SERBS PROCLAIM AUTONOMY
IN ANOTHER YUGOSLAV REGION

BOROUGH PARK WOMAN IS
SENTENCED IN THE FATAL
BEATING OF HER SON, 8

YELTSIN IN REBUFF TO UKRAINE
LAYS CLAIM TO BLACK SEA FLEET

Saturday, January 11, 1992
ISRAELI AIR RAID NEAR BEIRUT
KILLS 12

2 GET 25 YEARS TO LIFE IN
GAY MAN'S SLAYING IN QUEENS

TO THE PRESIDENTIAL HOPEFULS
THE MIDDLE CLASS IS ROYALTY

Sunday, January 13, 1992
ISRAELI SETTLERS SEE SHIFT
BY ARABS TO FIREARMS

TOKYO SEEKS TO PUNISH NETWORK
THAT TAPED BUSH

BIG SHELTERS HOLD TERRORS FOR
THE MENTALLY ILL

# 9

# THE CLOSING OF THE THEATER:
## *ECHOES OF JUSTICE*

When we were finally forced to abandon Third Street I guess nobody was really surprised. Given the history of the four other New York spaces taken away from The Living Theatre over the decades, the fact is that the Third Street venue lasted longer than all but 14th Street, which they held onto only six months longer.

The last production created at Third Street before the authorities stepped in was an exceptional event. Called *Echoes of Justice,* the play was a documentary drama drawn from court transcripts of the trial of Larry Davis, later Hakim, a black man accused of gunning down no less than six New York City police officers in a shootout. We came to produce it in a curious way.

During the time we were doing *The Body of God,* Judith, myself. and Exavier Wardlaw Muhammad, a fine theater artist and Lower East Side squatter who was a part of the Third Street company for most of the time we were there, did the late shift on Bob Fass' WBAI program. Bob was himself performing in *The Body of God* and we were eager to make the work known to the generally sympathetic listenership.

Among the calls that came in over the air was one from a pay phone at Rikers' Island prison. It was Hakim, saying, "If you mean what you say about using the theater as a tool to help fight injustice, you should do a play about me." And he told his version of the tale, how he was a street-wise kid recruited by cops on the take into a drug-dealing operation; how he tried to get out of the business and was hunted down by the policemen whom he could finger; how he shot his way out of a deadly ambush, managing to leave all six wounded cops alive. And how he has been beaten nearly to death repeatedly by jail guards.

We had no way of knowing how accurate his account was. Recurrent New York City police corruption scandals have repeatedly demonstrated that such things do happen in real life. The pain in Hakim's imprisoned voice was enough to send tears coursing down Exavier's cheeks, and in the following weeks, he did make contact with Hakim's attorney and got a hold of the trial transcripts. From these he adapted and directed a superbly crafted drama acted by a cast of neighborhood activist-artists capable of bringing to the theater the kind of reality that only a deeply passionate commitment to the material can produce. Exavier recruited a cast with real acting skill, including Bob Fass himself, and Charas organizer Bimbo Rivas, who died suddenly during the run of the play. Along one wall of the theater, there was a re-creation of the WBAI studio where Hakim had reached us. The other two walls were courtroom and tenements; street scenes were played in the aisles. It was a production that Erwin Piscator would have considered exemplary of his concept of political theater.

The play opened on the very evening of the riots in south-central Los Angeles that followed the acquittal of the policemen accused of beating Rodney King. The confluence of art and history gave the performances a stinging urgency that kept them fresh throughout the six-week run.

But soon after, a late-night avant-garde music performance that we are told involved the destruction of a washing machine with sledge hammers (J and I were in Calabria with *The Zero Method* when this happened) drove a distraught neighbor to call the police down on us. And it came to be discovered that the landlord did not possess a valid certificate of occupancy. The Buildings Department was notified and we were told that we could use the space for our own private purposes, but not allow public entry unless costly alterations were made. We met and talked and reluctantly came to the consensus that the financial burden of supporting the space had grown dangerously onerous. Either we would take on significant debt, or give up the ship to save the crew. We bailed out. We gave the summer over to a second series of *Waste* performances in various parks and streets. We had a going-out-of-business sale, and a valedictory three-week reprise of *The Zero Method*. We moved everything that remained — sets, costumes, archives, and the cartons of personal belongings of the no-fixed-address among us to a warehouse in Paterson, New Jersey.

We held a closing night party on the last day of January, 1993, before surrendering the keys. At the close of the evening I attempted to remove from its window mounting the yellow neon Living Theatre sign that Rudi Stern had made for us. My grip slipped and the mounting wire speared my hand. I spent the remainder of closing night alone at St. Vincent's, waiting two hours for a platoon of overcome firemen to be treated for smoke inhalation before the emergency room personnel could be troubled about a perforated finger.

The Living Theatre has been turned out of its rented quarters on Wooster Street (1948), Commerce Street (1953), West 100th Street (1956), West 14th Street (1963) and East 3rd Street (1993). But The Living Theatre Company, that ever-changing agglomeration of visionary theater artists, has remained. Fifteen years have passed at this writing from the time we were turned out of Third Street. To describe the intense activity that has characterized this period would be a book in itself. We have created an array of new works since then: several plays I've written, including *Anarchia* (1993), *Utopia* (1995), *Capital Changes* (1998), *Resistenza* (2000), *Resist Now!* (2001) as well as a version of *The Memoirs of Glückl of Hameln* which Joanie Fritz Zosike and I adapted together and presented first at the LaMama Galleria, and later at the Jewish Museum, under the title *And Then the Heavens Closed*.... Then, in 1997, the group devised a collective creation directed by Tom Walker at Theater for the New City (Crystal Field and, in the early years, George Bartenieff, the animating spirits at TNC, have been wonderfully hospitable to us over the many years) while Judith and I were busy doing workshops and other projects in Europe.

And for ten years now, we've been out in Times Square with *Not In My Name*, a protest play against the death penalty written by Judith, which we perform on days that someone is being executed in the United States.

In the years since we left Third Street, Europe has once again became the principal source of the company's livelihood as well as the place where we meet our largest and most enthusiastic audiences. Since leaving the Lower East Side, The Living Theatre has made repeated forays into Italy, Germany, France, Denmark, Portugal, Poland, Hungary, Bosnia, Serbia, Slovenia, Brazil, South Korea, and Lebanon. Nowhere, however, is appreciation of our work as consistently keen as it is in Italy, where in 1999, we opened the Centro Living Europa, which occupies the upper stories of a Palazzo Spinola built in 1650, and which we were able to renovate to our specifications to contain rooms for fourteen actors, an apartment for Judith and myself, rehearsal space, kitchen, baths, meeting rooms, and a performance space downstairs. But by 2003, the weight of events around the world and the heavy responsibility of the American government and economic interests for the state of war that reigns at present, convinced us that the time had come to take a stand in our native New York, heart of the imperial enterprise. So we sold the West End Avenue apartment we inherited from Julian's family.

After a deal gone bad scuttled plans for a space in Hell's Kitchen, we managed to find a large basement on the Lower East Side that suits our purposes beautifully. We signed a renewable ten-year lease, hired a contractor, and transformed an empty cellar into a beautiful performing space which opened the new Living Theatre on April 19, 2007 with a revival of Kenneth H. Brown's *The Brig*. The neon sign made by Rudi Stern, whom we lost recently to lung cancer, that hung for years in our Third Street window now fills the transom above the door to our new home at 21 Clinton Street.

So perhaps we'll still be able to pass on the torch here in Paul Goodman's Empire City, and searching young spirits of further generations will come to know our peculiar blend of art and zeal first-hand. The essential goal at Third Street was the goal we are pursuing now — to create a space suited to that particular encounter of actor, audience, and the idea of freedom that we call Living Theatre.

Fig. 21  New Music Flyer

# APPENDIX

## Chronological List of Events, Living on Third Street

APRIL 1989
4/19 Living Theatre Seder
4/21 Feldenkrais workshop
4/22–23 Carlo Altomare's and Elena Jandova's Bio-Mechanics Workshop
4/25 play reading: *Dems and U*s by John Farris

MAY 1989
5/26 *Tablets*, first preview
5/31 *Tablet*s opens, closes 7/2/89

AUGUST 1989
8/5–6, 8/19–20 *Tumult* performances, Prospect Park, Brooklyn
8/12, 8/27 *Tumult*, Green Oasis Community Garden, E. 8th St. bet. Aves. C & D, Manhattan
8/13 *Tumult*, Snug Harbor Cultural Center, Staten Island
8/21, 8/28 (see also Sept. and Oct. 1989) Living Jazz Festival, Austin John Marshall, director
8/27 *Tumult*, E. 6th St. and Ave. B Community Garden, Manhattan
8/29 Reading: Carmen Valle

SEPTEMBER 1989
9/2 *Tumult* performance, Tompkins Square Park, Manhattan
9/8 *IandI*, first preview
9/11, 9/18, 9/25 Living Jazz Festival (see also Aug. and Oct. 1989)
9/20 *IandI* opens, closes 2/11/90

OCTOBER 1989
10/2 Living Jazz Festival (see also Aug. and Sept. 1989)
10/10 Poetry reading: Living Theatre poets: Judith Malina, Hanon Reznikov, Tom Walker, Ilion Troya, Pamela Mayo, Steve Ben Israel, and others
10/17 Poetry reading: Taylor Mead and Penny Arcade
10/24 Poetry reading: Bob Rosenthal, Martin Matz, and Herbert Huncke
10/31 Poetry reading: Downtown Poets: Dorothy Friedman, Tuli Kupferberg,

Steve Taylor, Ellen Aug, Donald Lev, Enid Dame, Jim Feast, Bertha Rogers, and others

NOVEMBER 1989
11/7 Poetry reading: Katherine Texier, Joel Rose, and Patrick McGrath
11/17 *Tablets* re-opens in repertory, closes 1/28/90
11/28 Poetry reading: Armand Schwerner and Michael Heller

DECEMBER 1989
12/5 Poetry reading: Erika Duncan, Hilda Morley, Jean Valentine, Meena Alexander
12/12 Reading: Ken Brown and Ira Cohen
12/19 Poetry reading: Jerome Rothenberg with Charles Morrow and Judith Malina

JANUARY 1990
1/21 Play reading: *Orpheus* by Exavier Wardlaw Muhammad
1/28 Play reading: *The Demise of the Egotist,* Johann Fatzer by Bertolt Brecht

FEBRUARY 1990
2/13 Meeting: Living Theatre Job Branch of the IWW (Industrial Workers of the World)
2/27 Meeting: IWW

MARCH 1990
3/27 Poetry reading: Jackson Mac Low, Nick Piombino, and Charles Bernstein
3/28 *Body of God* opens, closes 4/22/90

APRIL 1990
4/3 John Farris and Norman Douglas
4/9 Living Theatre Seder
4/17 An Evening of Storytelling: Spencer Holst, Vit Horejs, and Garrick Beck
4/23 "Shut Down Wall Street" demonstration, first public performance of Wobbly Chorus (Living Theatre IWW singing group, Michael Shenker, director)

MAY 1990
5/1 Poetry reading: David Trinidad, Susan Wheeler, and David Lehman
5/9 *German Requiem* opens, closes 7/1/90
5/12 Meeting: IWW
5/15 Poetry reading: Kenneth H. Brown, Ira Cohen, and Valery Oistenau
5/22 Poetry reading: Allen Ginsberg Living Theatre benefit
5/28 Performance: *The Innocent* by Technotribe Stomp

JUNE 1990
6/19 Poetry reading: Judith Malina, Hanon Reznikov, Taylor Mead, Dorothy
    Friedman, Gary Azon, Stephen Paul Miller, Patrick Christiano, Nina Zi-
    vancevic, Zoe Anglesey, Sharon Mesmer, John Farris, and others

JULY 1990
7/4 Meeting: IWW. Wobbly Chorus performance at East River Park,
    Manhattan
7/14 *IandI* opens in Chieri, Italy
7/17 *Tablets* opens in Chieri
7/18 Workshop street performance: "Apathy and Action," Chieri
7/22 Augsburg, Germany: workshop performance — "Nationalism is Racism"
7/30 *Tablets* opens in Malaga, Spain

AUGUST 1990
8/6–7 *El Puente de Wirikuta* wih Fantuzzi and the Flexible Band
8/9 *IandI* opens in Berlin
8/15 *Tablets* opens in Berlin
8/17 Living Theatre Cabaret midnight performance in Berlin
8/19 Workshop street performance "A Day in the Life of the City," Berlin

Fig. 22  Poetry Reading Flyer

8/21 Prague, Czechoslovakia: workshop street performance,
   "A Day in the Life of the City," Prague
8/22 *Tablets* opens in Brno, Czechoslovakia
8/23 Workshop street performance, Brno
8/24 *IandI* opens in Brno

SEPTEMBER 1990
9/1 *German Requiem* reopens Living Theatre at Third Street, closes 9/9/90
9/2 *Tablets* opens in L'Aquila, Italy
9/6–7 Arezzo: workshop street performance "A Day in the Life of the City"
9/22 Performance: Divine Monochord by Iris Lord with Ira Cohen
   and Copernicus
9/25 IWW potluck dinner
9/29 Concert

OCTOBER 1990
10/1 Play reading: *Shame* by Duggan, with George McGrath
10/2 Dance workshop performance, Johnson Anthony, director
10/5–7, 10/9 Performance: *Many Shades of Fade* by Echnaton
10/8 Play reading: Marshall Berman, author
10/9 Meeting: IWW
10/17 *Body of God* reopens, closes 11/11
10/22 Play reading: Tom Lavazzi, author
10/23 Poetry reading: Hanon Reznikov, Judith Malina, Joanie Fritz Zosike,
   Henry Freeman, Bobby Heiger, Martin Reckhaus, Tom Walker,
   and others

NOVEMBER 1990
11/1 Play reading: John Farris
11/5 Play reading: *Self Destruct*
11/14 New Director's Series: *The Maids* by Jean Genet opens,
   Erica Bilder, director, closes 12/5/90
11/20 Reading, from his autobiography *Guilty of Everything:* Herbert Huncke
11/27 Reading, from his *One Thousand Avant Garde Plays:* Kenneth Koch

DECEMBER 1990
12/3 Play reading: *Plunder*
12/4 Poetry reading: David Ignatow, Mark Rudman, and Virginia Terris
12/9 Concert: Patrick Grant, composer and director
12/17 Dance concert: "House of Johnson," Johnson Anthony,
   director and choreographer

JANUARY 1991
1/13 Anti-Gulf War demonstration performance, United Nations
1/15 Poetry reading: Nina Zivancevic and Amiel Alcalay

FEBRUARY 1991
2/6 *Rules of Civility*, first preview Living Theatre at Third Street,
    opens 2/13/91, closes 4/21/91
2/12 Poetry reading: Ofelia Rodriguez-Goldstein, Kimberly Browne,
    Audrey Alenson
2/19 *Rules of Civility* opens Rome, Italy
2/26 *Rules of Civility*, Salerno, Italy
2/27 *Rules of Civility*, Naples, Italy

MARCH 1991
3/5 *Rules of Civility*, Torino, Italy
3/11 *Rules of Civility*, Moncalieri, Italy
3/14 *Rules of Civility*, Cagliari, Italy
3/19 Poetry reading: Daisy Aldan and Geronimo Sands
3/21 *Rules of Civility*, Urbino, Italy
3/23 *Rules of Civility*, Padua, Italy
3/24 Workshop street performance: Padua
3/27 *Rules of Civility*, Marano sul Panaro, Italy
3/29 *Rules of Civility*, Budapest, Hungary

APRIL 1991
4/2 *Rules of Civility*, Szekesfehervar
4/9 Poetry reading: Ricardo Pau-Llosa and Dionisio Martinez

MAY 1991
5/29 New Director Series: *Humanity* by Walter Hasenclever,
    Elena Jandova and Martin Reckhaus, directors, closes 6/30/91

JUNE 1991
6/5 Poetry reading: Ron Kolm, Max Blagg, and Lynne Tillman

JULY 1991
7/1 Play reading: Mac Wellman, author
7/27 *Waste Museum* opens, closes 8/28/91

AUGUST 1991
8/2 *Waste* opens at 7th St. Recycling Center, Manhattan
8/3 *Waste*, East River Park, Manhattan
8/4 *Waste*, Plaza Cultural, 9th St. and Ave. C, Manhattan

8/10 *Waste,* Washington Square Park, Manhattan
8/11 *Waste,* Union Square Pavilion, Manhattan
8/17 *Waste,* Williamsburg/Greenpoint, Brooklyn
8/18 *Waste:* Prospect Park, Brooklyn
8/24 *Waste:* 7th St. Recycling Center, Manhattan
8/25 *Waste* closes at 3rd St.

SEPTEMBER 1991
9/4 New Director Series: *Beirut* by Alan Bowne,
    Christina Kirk, director, closes 9/29/91
9/15 Berlin: workshop street performance "A Day in the Life of the City"

OCTOBER 1991
10/4–5, 10/11–12, 10/18–19 Bob Paton's *Theatre of Dreams*
10/6, 10/13, 10/20 Performance: Sophia Wycherly
10/22 Poetry reading: Downtown Newspaper Poets: Richard Chase,
    Diana Cohen, Phil Demise/Phil Smith, Marilyn Lippel, and others
10/24–27 Dance concert: "House of Johnson,"
    Johnson Anthony, director and choreographer

NOVEMBER 1991
11/1–11/3 Performance: *Traveling Woman* by Nadime Nader,
    author, director, choreographer
11/1 Poetry reading: Irving Wexler, Carlotta Joy Walker, and Robert Roth
11/19 Bob Paton's *Theatre of Dreams*
11/21 New Director Series: *Death Watch* by Jean Genet opens,
    Kris Cuppens, director, closes 12/6/91

DECEMBER 1991
12/3 Poetry reading: The New Feminists: Denise Duhamel,
    Diane Spodarek, Bina Sharif, Jackie Johnson, and Susan Sherman
12/5 40th Anniversary Benefit at Cooper Union,
    with first performance of Zero *Method*
12/7 Performance: by Kush
12/10 Bob Paton's *Theatre of Dreams*
12/17 Reading: Emerging Downtown Writers: Romy Ashby, Patrick Christiano,
    David Huberman, Jose Padua, J.D. Rage, Janet Restino and others
12/27 *Zero Method* opens, closes 1/12/92

JANUARY 1992
1/8 Reading: Colette Inez and others
1/12 Living Theatre Cabaret
1/17 New Director Series: *We Should…(a lie)*

by Kenneth Bernard, director, Robert Press
1/26–27 *Zero Method* opens Modena, Italy

FEBRUARY 1992
2/7–9 *Zero Method*, Cosenza
2/8 Workshop street performance: Cosenza
2/11–16 *Zero Method*, Napoli
2/13 Workshop street performance: Napoli
2/19–24 *Zero Method*, Palermo
2/24 Workshop street performance: Palermo
2/26–3/1 *Zero Method*, Cagliani

MARCH 1992
3/6–7 *Zero Method*, Pontedera
3/11–12 *Zero Method*, Longiano
3/13 *Zero Method*, Forli
3/14–15 *Zero Method*, Bologna
3/17 *Zero Method*, Albano
3/19 *Zero Method*, Latina
3/20 *Zero Method*, Aprilia
3/21 *Zero Method*, L'Aquila
3/24–29 *Zero Method*, Torino
3/30 Franco Quadri's Retrospective of the 1950s: scenes from *The Marrying Maiden* by Jackson Mac Low and *Desire Trapped by the Tail* by Pablo Picasso

APRIL 1992
4/1–3 *Zero Method*, Genoa (Sestri)
4/4 Performance: *The Set-Up* by Steve Cannon, director, Norman Douglas
4/7 Staged reading: *Semi-Permeable Membranes/ Enigmas in a Labyrinth* by Julian Beck, director, Ilion Troya
4/11–12 Dance performance by Patricia Winter
4/14 Reading: Ninotchka Rosca
4/24 Poetry reading: Jack Micheline
4/30 *Echoes of Justice* opens, director, Exavier Wardlaw Muhammad, closes 6/6/92

JUNE 1992
6/7 Poetry reading: Lloyd Van Brunt, Julia Kasdorf, and Juanita Brunk
6/20 *Waste* reopens: 3rd St., closes 8/2/92
6/21 *Waste:* Union Square, Manhattan
6/28 *Waste:* Plaza Cultural, 9th St. and Ave. C, Manhattan

JULY 1992
7/5 *Waste:* Chrystie St., Manhattan

7/10–11 Dance performance by Patricia Winter
7/12 *Waste:* 125 St., Manhattan
7/18 *Waste:* Greenpoint, Brooklyn
7/19 *Waste:* Pitts Street, Manhattan
7/25 *Waste:* Plaza Cultural, Manhattan
7/26 *Waste:* 3rd St.

AUGUST 1992
8/1 *Waste:* Union Square, Manhattan
8/2 *Waste:* 3rd St.
8/17 Reading: Alvin Eng's "More Stories from the Pagan Pagoda," director, Robert Press
8/25 Play reading: *Runaways* by Steve Hager

SEPTEMBER 1992
9/2 *Zero Method* reopens, closes 9/26/92
9/22 Reading: "Candy Darling" with Taylor Mead, Gregory Corso, Ira Cohen, Penny Arcade, and others

OCTOBER 1992
10/1–3, 10/8–10, 10/15–17 New Choreographer's Showcase: House of Johnson, Johnson Anthony and others
10/18–19, 10/25–26 New Music Series: Sound Minds, organized by Patrick Grant (see Nov. 1992)

NOVEMBER 1992
11/8–9 New Music Series: Sound Minds (see Oct. 1992)

# BIOGRAPHICAL NOTES

BEATE HEIN BENNETT, born and raised in Germany, is a teacher, freelance dramaturge, and translator, living in New York City. She holds a Ph.D. in Comparative Literature, and has worked in theatre in Germany and the US. She was happy to bring *IandI* to The Living Theatre.

JUDITH MALINA with Julian Beck, founded The Living Theatre in 1947. As director, actor, and producer, she is responsible for bringing nearly a hundred anarchist-pacifist plays to audiences around the world.

HANON REZNIKOV met The Living Theatre while a student at Yale in 1968. Following the death of Julian Beck in 1985, he directed the company alongside Judith Malina. During the two decades before Reznikov's death in 2008, he also wrote many of the group's plays.

CINDY ROSENTHAL is Associate Professor of Drama and Dance and Director of Women's Studies at Hofstra University. She has worked extensively as a performer and a writer and co-edited *Restaging the Sixties: Radical Theatres and Their Legacies*.

# INDEX OF NAMES

Aedem
Ellen Stewart, Leo Castelli, Penny Arcade
Karen Malpede, Sheila Dabney (a "dazzlingly accomplished actor")

TNC

The Magic Theater San Francisco